C000067927

THE APOCALYPSE OF ELIJAH

Society of Biblical Literature

 TEXTS AND TRANSLATIONS
PSEUDEPIGRAPHA SERIES

Harold W. Attridge, Editor

Texts and Translations 19
Pseudepigrapha Series 9

THE APOCALYPSE OF ELIJAH
based on
P. CHESTER BEATTY 2018

by
Albert Pietersma
and
Susan Turner Comstock
with
Harold W. Attridge

THE APOCALYPSE OF ELIJAH
based on
P. CHESTER BEATTY 2018

coptic text edited and translated by
Albert Pietersma
and
Susan Turner Comstock
with
Harold W. Attridge

Scholars Press

THE APOCALYPSE OF ELIJAH
based on
P. CHESTER BEATTY 2018
by
Albert Pietersma
and
Susan Turner Comstock
with
Harold W. Attridge

Copyright © 1981
Society of Biblical Literature

Library of Congress Cataologing in Publication Data

Bible, O.T. Apocryphal books. Apocalypse of Elijah. Coptic. 1979.

The apocalypse of Elijah.

(Pseudepigrapha series; 9 ISSN 0145-3238) (Texts and translations—Society of Biblical Literature; 19 ISSN 0145-3203).
    In English and Coptic; introductory matter in English.
    Coptic text reproduced from ms. copy.
    Includes bibliographical references and indexes.
    I. Pietersma, Albert. II. Comstock, Susan Turner. III. Attridge, Harold W. IV. Chester Beatty Library. MSS—(Pap. 2018) V. Bible. O.T. Apocryphal books. Apocalypse of Elijah. English. 1979 VI. Title. VII. Series. VIII. Series: Society of Biblical Literature. Texts and translations; 19.
BS1830.E45C66 1979 229'.913   79-24788
ISBN 0-89130-371-5
ISBN 0-89130-373-1 pbk.

Printed in the United States of America

TEXTS AND TRANSLATIONS is a project of the Committee on Research
and Publications of the Society of Biblical Literature and is under
the general direction of Kent H. Richards (Iliff School of Theology),
Executive Secretary and Leander Keck (Yale Divinity School), Chairman of the Committee. The purpose of the project is to make avail-
able in convenient and inexpensive format ancient texts which are not
easily accessible but are of importance to scholars and students of
"biblical literature" as broadly defined by the Society. Reliable
modern English translations will accompany the texts. The following
subseries have been established thus far:

> PSEUDEPIGRAPHA, edited by
>> Harold W. Attridge (Southern Methodist University)
> GRECO-ROMAN RELIGION, edited by
>> Hans Dieter Betz (University of Chicago)
>> Edward N. O'Neil (University of Southern California)
> EARLY CHRISTIAN LITERATURE, edited by
>> Robert L. Wilken (University of Notre Dame)
>> William R. Schoedel (University of Illinois)

For the PSEUDEPIGRAPHA SERIES the choice of texts is governed in
part by the research interests of the SBL Pseudepigrapha Group, of
which John J. Collins (De Paul University) is currently Chairman, and
James H. Charlesworth (Duke University) is Secretary. This series will
focus on Jewish materials from the Hellenistic and Greco-Roman periods
and will regularly include the fragmentary evidence of works attributed
to biblical personalities, culled from a wide range of Jewish and
Christian sources. The volumes are selected, prepared, and edited in
consultation with the following editorial committee of the Pseudepigrapha Group: Sebastian P. Brock (Cambridge University, England) Robert
A. Kraft (University of Pennsylvania) George W. MacRae (Harvard Divinity
School) George W. E. Nickelsburg, Jr. (University of Iowa) Michael E.
Stone (Hebrew University, Israel) John Strugnell (Harvard Divinity
School).

The current volume differs from the other volumes heretofore published in this series, since it constitutes the *editio princeps* of a major manuscript witness to the *Apocalypse of Elijah*. Hence, it has seemed desirable to provide a fuller textual apparatus than is normally offered in this series, as well as photographic plates of Papyrus Chester Beatty 2018 and of the Greek fragment of the Apocalypse.

Harold W. Attridge, Editor

FOREWORD

The *editio princeps* of P. Chester Beatty inv. 2018 was made possible by a Research Grant from the Social Sciences and Humanities Research Council of Canada which enabled me during the summer of 1977 to study the manuscript first hand. I wish to express to the Council my sincere thanks and appreciation for their generous assistance.

To the Chester Beatty Library and Gallery of Oriental Art, Dublin, I am grateful for the kind permission granted me to publish this important manuscript of the Library's collection. In a special way, I owe a debt of gratitude to the Islamic Curator, Mr. David James who both professionally and socially has, on so many occasions, made my stays in Dublin eminently profitable and enjoyable. In recognition and with gratefulness this volume has been dedicated to him and his wife Verna, who always makes their home such a pleasant place to visit.

My friend and fellow editor Dr. Susan Comstock has shared in all the work that the present book has entailed. If it had not been for her readiness to undertake the venture, this volume would not have come into being. My gratitude to her is more than I can express.

The Editor of the Pseudepigrapha Texts and Translations, Dr. Harold W. Attridge, has gone far beyond his official duties as Editor of the Series. For his multifarious contributions to the book he has more than earned his name on the title page.

Albert Pietersma

University of Toronto

August 1979

To David and Verna

ERRATA

Page 5, line 6 (from bottom): "mistake" should read "mistakes"

Page 20, line 12 (from bottom): "ⲕⲟⲩⲕⲥ̄" should read "ⲛⲟⲩⲕⲥ̄"

Page 41, line 22: a comma should follow "blows"

Page 46, line 2: "ϩⲓ[ⲟⲏ" should read "ϩⲓ[ⲑⲏ"

Page 52, line 16: "ⲛⲁ·ⲟ[ⲅⲟⲏⲟⲩ" should read "ⲛⲁ·ⲟ[ⲅⲟⲙⲟⲩ"

TABLE OF CONTENTS

SIGLA AND ABBREVIATIONS

Ach Gk Sa^1 Sa^2 Sa^3	see Introd. p. 1
c	corrected reading (in manuscript)
inc	incertum (uncertain reading of ms.)
om	omit(s)
pr	preceded by
tr (post)	transposed (after)
vid	ut videtur (apparent reading of ms.)
vs.	versus
.	uncertain letter
= (in app. crit.)	equivalent (but not identical) reading
*	original reading (of ms.)
< >	editors' addition
{ }	editors' deletion
[ ]	editors' reconstruction
⟦ ⟧	scribal deletion
>	resulting in
<	resulting from
↑	verso side (of folio)
→	recto side (of folio)
1° etc.	first occurrence etc.

INTRODUCTION

The manuscripts:

Berlin, staatl. Museen, Abteilung P. 1862. Six folios [Steindorff 21-26, 35-36, 41-44], in the Achmimic dialect. III/IV century. Papyrus. Edition: Georg Steindorff, *Die Apokalypse des Elias, eine unbekannte Apokalypse und Bruchstücke der Sophonias - Apokalypse, koptische Texte, Übersetzung, Glossar* (Texte und Untersuchungen zur Geschichte der altchristlichen Literatur, Neue Folge. II. Band, Heft 3a), Leipzig 1899. For Achmimic 39, 13-17 and 40, 12-16 see Carl Schmidt, "Der Kolophon ..." p. 321, cited below.

Dublin, Chester Beatty Library and Gallery of Oriental Art, 2018 (Acc 1493). Ten folios, in the Sahidic dialect. IV/V century. Papyrus.

London, British Museum or. 7594 (colophon). Forty one lines, in the Sahidic dialect. IV century. Papyrus. Edition: Carl Schmidt, "Der Kolophon des Ms. orient 7594 des Britischen Museums. Eine Untersuchung zur Elias-Apokalypse," *Sitzungsberichte der Preussischen Akademie der Wissenschaften* (Philosophisch-Historische Klasse), Berlin 1925, pp. 312-321.

Paris, Bibliothèque Nat., Copte 135. Seven folios [Steindorff 19-20, 27-34, 37-40] in the Achmimic dialect. III/IV century. Papyrus. Six folios [Steindorff 3-14] in the Sahidic dialect. IV/V century. Papyrus. Edition: Steindorff, *op. cit.*

Florence, Biblioteca Medicea Laurenziana, PSI 7. Fragment of 6.5 x 6.5 cm, in Greek. IV century. Papyrus. Editions: E. Pistelli in *Papiri greci e latini* (Pubblicazioni della Società Italiana), vol. 1. Florence 1912, no. 7, pp. 16-17; A. Pietersma, "The Greek *Apocalypse of Elijah*," Appendix of present monograph.

The following abbreviations for the MSS have been employed: Ach = the Achmimic text, Sa^1 = the Sahidic text of Paris, Sa^2 = the Sahidic colophon text, Sa^3 = the Sahidic text of Chester Beatty, and Gk = PSI 7.

Papyrus Chester Beatty 2018

1.   The manuscript

    P. Chester Beatty 2018 consists of ten folios, the first five of which are virtually complete, while the remainder is in somewhat more fragmentary condition but was skillfully reassembled into its present state by Mr. A. F. Shore, formerly of the British Museum, who in 1958 wrote a brief accompanying note for the manuscript. A total of sixty seven unplaced fragments were collected into a separate frame. The majority of these, however, we were subsequently able to place and re-unite with the manuscript before the final photographs were made. Three of the remaining fragments perhaps deserve brief comment:

1

a.6↑ and a.7↑ may belong on page TH̄ (18) lines 13-14 to read (N̄) ϥκε-
(λεγε) and (τ)λλ(γ) respectively. But since this creates serious
difficulties on the recto side of that folio (τζ̄ (17) lines 12-14)
these two pieces were left among the unplaced. Further, b.5↑ (ϭ and
x) may have the initial letters of lines 1 and 2 of page ζ̄ (7) with
μ of (H̄)μ(λγ) page H̄ (8) line 2 on the recto side. But again, a
number of problems preclude positive identification.

The pages of our manuscript were numbered λ̄-κ̄ (1-20) with the
following pagination extant in whole or in part: Ḇ Ḡ λ̄ ē ϭ̄ ζ̄ H̄
ē τ τλ̄ τλ̄ τϭ̄ τH̄. The leaves formed, apparently, a single quire
of five bifolios, though no conjugate leaves have survived. In the
first half of the quire, (λ̄-τ), verso precedes recto, while the reverse
is true for pages τλ̄-κ̄. Though no page has been preserved in its
original size, it is clear from what remains that the manuscript had
ample margins. The largest extant leaf (fol. 4) measures 16.7 x 19.9
cm *in toto,* with upper and lower margins measuring, at their widest
points, 2.6 cm (fol. 8→) and 2 cm (fol. 4↑) respectively. Righthand
and lefthand margins are 3.4 cm (fol. 7→) and 2.8 cm (fol. 1↑). The
text of the manuscript was written in a single column of approximately
14 x 17 cm in size. Whereas the lefthand side of the column is reasonably straight, the righthand side tends to be jagged in places.
Lines of writing per column number anywhere from 18 (p. 7) to 24 (p. 1),
and spacing between lines varies considerably. Good examples of this
variation are furnished by folio 3→ and folio 6→. The number of letters per line may fluctuate between 19 and 30, but usually lines con-
sist of 24-26 letters.

An interesting feature of P. Chester Beatty 2018 is its sys-
tem of punctuation marks which is apparently original to the manuscript.
In addition to supralineation as a mark of syllabicity, which one
usually encounters in Coptic manuscripts, a raised point or dot is
employed in our manuscript to mark syllabic division while a raised,
slanted stroke (') sets off (usually) larger lexical units which may
vary in length from a single morpheme (cf. e.g. 'ïωτ' 2,2) to whole
clauses. Dot and stroke are mutually exclusive, but on occasion the
scribe appears to have changed his mind as to which was appropriate
in a given instance. To cite but one example, in 8,3 we now have
H̄˙ⲡⲉγ˙ʹH˙ⲉⲓ˙ʹ . Evidently the scribe meant to write H̄˙ⲡⲉγ˙H˙ⲉⲓʹ,

but by mistake placed a dot where he should have used a stroke.
Attempting to correct his first error he committed a second one by
placing the stroke first after ⲙ̄ and only then where it belongs,
namely after ⲙ̄ⲡⲉⲩⲏⲉⲓ. It needs to be stressed, however, that
although dot and stroke are mutually exclusive, it is by no means
clear in every instance which is to be read, since the scribe's frequently elongated dots look at times remarkably like his strokes.
Again a few examples will illustrate the difficulty. In 10,10 we
read ⲉⲩ·ⲁⲓ·ⲭⲙⲁ·ⲗⲱ·ⲧⲓ·ⲍⲉ′ where the dot after ⲁⲓ is elongated and
could be read as a stroke - which is hardly intended. In 16,6 we have
ⲍⲙ̄·ⲙⲉⲍ·ϥ[ⲧ]ⲟ′ⲟⲩ′. How is this to be read? What separates ⲧⲟ and
ⲟⲩ must surely be intended as a dot but could easily be read as a
stroke. More difficult to interpret, however, is the mark at the end
of this phrase. Either stroke or dot would make sense and either can
be read! A further noteworthy fact is that dots are not all formed
in the same way. In addition to the dots that resemble the familiar
slanted stroke, one also finds, for example, short vertical strokes
(') and short diagonal strokes formed from left to right (`). As one
might expect, neither the dot nor the stroke is used with absolute
consistency, though in the case of the former the degree of consistency is remarkable. As an example of inconsistency in this connection
one might cite ⲛⲏ·ⲥⲧⲓ·ⲁ in 3,15. In the two other fully extant
occurrences of this word we find a different division ⲛⲉⲥ·ⲧⲓ·ⲁ (3,3)
and again ⲛⲏⲥ·ⲧⲓ·ⲁ (3,11). Greater inconsistency exists in the
use of the stroke. Let us take as an example the rather frequently
occurring phrase "at that time" expressed either in a plural or singular construction: ⲍⲛ̄ⲛⲉⲍⲟⲟⲩ/ⲍⲙ̄ⲡⲉⲍⲟⲟⲩ ⲉⲧⲙ̄ⲙⲁⲩ. Ten times in our
manuscript it occurs without a stroke separating the two main consti-
tuent elements (5,15; 6,1; 7,10.13; 9,9; 10,8.19; 18,4.15.21) but
twice we find it with a stroke before ⲉⲧⲙ̄ⲙⲁⲩ, without any apparent
difference in meaning being intended.

In addition to supralineation, dots and strokes, we find diaeresis
on final, medial and initial iota and once on medial upsilon
(ⲡⲉⲛⲧⲁϥⲧⲁⲙⲓⲉⲧⲏⲩ̈ⲧⲛ̄ 1,6). Interestingly, in the vast majority of
cases the diaeresis is employed together with the supralinear dot.
Thus we find ⲁ·ⲱⲁ·ï (2,19); (ⲉ·)ⲍⲣⲁ·ï (1,14; 2,14; 5,12; 7,8.9;
8,12; 9,5.8.9; 10,2.11; 11,11; 14,13; 17,8; 18,6.14); [ⲗⲟⲩⲁ]ⲁ·ï

(17,1); ⲛⲁ·ⲓ̈ (1,2; 3,1.7; 18,4); ⲛⲓ·ⲟⲩ·ⲭⲁ·ⲓ̈ (10,10); ⲡⲁ·ⲓ̈ (1,18; 13,16; 14,7; 16,10; 18,10); ⲡⲉ·ⲓ̈ (16,15); ⲧⲁ·ⲓ̈ (12,19); ⲟⲩ·ⲭⲁ·ⲓ̈ (15,1.7);]ⲟⲩ·ⲓ̈ (6,19). However, we also encounter (ⲉ·)ⲉⲣⲁ̈ⲓ̈ (5,18; 12,6.7); ⲧⲁⲓ̈ (4,18). Instances of diaeresis on medial iota are ⲡⲁ·ⲓ̈·ⲱⲧ (7,18) and ⲧⲁ·ⲓ̈·ⲏ·ⲟⲩ· (3,7), and on initial iota ⲓ̈·ⲱⲧ (2,2).

A raised comma or apostrophe appears after final gamma (9,14), medial gamma (4,2.21; 9,16; 19,14), final kappa (9,3; 15,4.6; 17,13; 18,5; 19,10; 20,17), final lambda (17,6; 18,1), final tau (1,4.16; 2,2; 3,4.6.7.11.16; 4,1.5.19.20; 5,2.2.10.17.18; 6,3.17; 7,9.18; 9,2.6.18.19; 10,9.19; 11,1.2.11; 12,3.6; 13,15; 14,17.18; 15,10; 17,4.11; 18,3.6.10), medial tau (3,5.8; 4,12; 8,16; 9,1; 10,4; 11,8; 13,9.10; 14,17; 15,3; 16,8; 17,13.17; 18,12); † 20,14. Like the diaeresis, the apostrophe is followed by either a raised dot or raised stroke, but, since the latter are mutually exclusive, never by both.

Abbreviation of the *nomina sacra* is limited to ⲭⲣⲓⲥⲧⲟⲥ>ⲭ̅ⲥ̅ (12,10.12; 18,13; 19,5; 20,5.9), and ⲡⲛⲉⲩⲙⲁ>ⲡ̅ⲛ̅ⲁ̅ (17,14). Once, however, we find ⲭⲏⲥⲧⲟⲥ (13,14), and the full form has been reconstructed in 18,22 *spatii causa*. It is possible, of course, that in the latter instance Sa[3] had a plus, but neither Sa[1] nor Ach lends support to this assumption.

The Chester Beatty *Apocalypse of Elijah* was written on what Mr. Shore described as papyrus of a poor quality. Certainly quality leaves a good deal to be desired. Frequently one finds patches of twisted, chipped and missing fibers, and in spots the manuscript was left blank due to its inferior state. One might refer here to 2,11 where a hole in the papyrus forced the scribe to write ⲛ̅ ⲉⲓ, or again to 6,7 where a space equivalent to 4 or 5 letters was left blank because of a crack in the writing surface. Similarly in 7,3-4 we find blank spaces, and again in lines 15-18 of the same page. In line 16 of this passage the scribe intended to write ⲛⲉ(ⲧⲟⲩⲁⲁⲃ) contiguously but was forced by the surface to abandon his first effort to write ⲉ.

2. Scribal errors and corrections

On the whole P. Chester Beatty 2018 was carelessly written, and a considerable number of errors escaped detection by the copyist. Supralinear corrections, however, are frequent and vary in length from a single letter to a whole line which, due to parablepsis, had been left out. On page 1 the scribe's eye skipped from ⲉⲧⲙ̄ⲕⲁ (line 13f.) to the same word one line lower, with the result that the intervening words dropped out but were restored between the lines. A rather interesting instance of supra-linear correction occurs in 17,13. Initially the scribe apparently wrote ⲛ̄ⲟⲩⲁ ⲛ̄ⲟⲩⲁ instead of the required ⲛ̄ⲑⲉ ⲛ̄ⲟⲩⲁ. Realizing his mistake, he attempted to correct it - but apparently placed ⲛ̄ⲑⲉ above the second rather than the first ⲛ̄ⲟⲩⲁ. Possibly thoroughly disgusted with himself by now, the scribe at last introduced the appropriate correction, but with the result that his various efforts and the state of the manuscript have given us a somewhat jumbled text. Well attested also are instances of over-writing. Thus, for example, in 5,5 an original ⲉⲃⲟⲥ was corrected to ⲉⲃⲟⲗ. Twice, words which had been added due to dittography or because of a misreading of syntax were crossed out: 3,2 ϩⲏⲧⲟⲩ$^{2°}$ and 17, 5 ⲙ̄ⲛ̄. Sometimes a mistake was arrested but not crossed out. The most interesting example here is furnished by 10,11 where the scribe was about to write ϩⲛ̄ twice but realized his mistake in time and left us a partially written ϩ. Marginal additions are limited, as far as one can determine, to the upper and lower margins. In the lower margin of 7 we have ⲅⲁⲑⲟⲛ, and in the upper margins of pp. 14 and 18 one can read ⲛ̄[ϫⲱϥ] and ⲙⲉⲓ[ⲗ] respectively.

Before we leave this section an explanatory statement is in order. In the upper apparatus of the present edition a perhaps questionable approach has been followed. In addition to scribal corrections, all evidently *prima manu*, the reader might reasonably expect to find further corrections proposed by the editors. Indeed, a large number of obvious scribal errors could readily have been corrected, but, since in Coptic it is not always clear where mistakes end and orthographical variants begin, we have refrained from following such a route. Furthermore, the obvious mistake will present no problem to even amateur Coptologists, while the more ambiguous phenomena deserve more extensive treatment by experts than can be allotted to them in the present context. There is, moreover, good reason to believe that both the punctuation and orthography (among other things) of the new text will be subjected in the near future to the detailed scrutiny they deserve.

3. Date and text

On palaeographical grounds Mr. A. F. Shore, in the note to which
reference has been made above, dates the Chester Beatty *Apocalypse*
to the end of the fourth or the beginning of the fifth century A.D.
This date is corroborated by a comparison of our manuscript with the
most recent work on Coptic palaeography by Maria Cramer,[1] though perhaps the date is more nearly fifth century than fourth. If this date
is correct the Chester Beatty manuscript is of approximately the same
date as Bib. Nat. Copte 135 Sahidic (=Sa[1]) which has been variously
dated to the fourth (Rosenstiehl), fourth/fifth (Shore), and fifth
(Carl Schmidt) centuries, and is somewhat younger than both the Achmimic text of Berlin and Paris (third/fourth) and the colophon text of
the British Museum (fourth). One would do well to remember, however,
that dates based on palaeographical evidence alone are subject to a
substantial margin of error. The uncial script of our manuscript, or
rather its writing in *capitals* as E. G. Turner is wont to insist,[2] is
much closer in character and appearance to the script of Ach and the
semi-cursive of Sa[2] than to the more typical 'Coptic Uncial' of Sa[1].

The new manuscript of the *Apocalypse of Elijah* confirms what
scholars have long held and what the BM colophon text graphically
demonstrated for the first time, namely, that the Elijah apocalypse
constitutes a separate, independent work. Like Sa[2] but unlike Ach and
Sa[1] our manuscript begins (and ends) with the *Apocalypse of Elijah*.
It is surprising that the Chester Beatty manuscript ends abruptly in
the middle of the speech of "the lawless one," and the line fillers on
the concluding line of page 20 suggest that the abrupt termination is
not due to the vicissitudes of survival. At least the immediate
Vorlage of our manuscript must likewise have lacked the concluding
pages of the *Apocalypse*.

Before looking at the question of textual affiliation we should
perhaps remind ourselves of the fact that not a single one of the four
Coptic manuscripts of the *Apocalypse of Elijah* now at our disposal con-
tains the complete work, but with the fortunate addition of the Chester
Beatty manuscript we do now at last possess the complete *Apocalypse*,

---

[1] *Koptische Paläographie*, Wiesbaden 1964.
[2] Cf. *Greek Manuscripts of the Ancient World*, Princeton N.J. 1971, p. 1.

and in spite of the many variant readings that separate our four witnesses the unity of the textual tradition deserves to be emphasized.
Our most recently discovered witness to this tradition, P. Chester
Beatty 2018, apart from furnishing an impressive array of *variae
lectiones*, gives us thirty-four lines of text which were hitherto
unknown. Hence, with the help of our new manuscript and the results
of a re-examination of the codicology of the Achmimic manuscript by
Dr. Ibscher (see Carl Schmidt, *op. cit.*, p. 318) the *Apocalypse* as a
whole can now be pieced together as follows:

Sa³	Sa²	Sa¹	Ach
a. 1,1-4,16	1,1-2^b,17		19,1-24,4
b. 4,17-6,16		3,1-4,33	24,4-26,18
c. 6,16-8,14			
d. 8,14-13,4			27,1-32,14
e. 13,4-14,17		5,1-6,20	32,15-34,17
f. 14,17-16,8		6,20-7,35	
g. 16,8-20,16		7,35-13,11	35,1-40,16
h. 20,16-20,23		13,11-13,23	
i.		13,23-14,29	
j.		14,29-14,33	41,1-41,3
k.			41,3-44,2

In terms of contents this means:

Sa³1,1-4,16
Sa²1,1-2^b,17
Ach 19,1-24,4

I   The prophet receives his commission

II The seer exhorts the saints and reminds them
    of God's promises

    A.   The addressees are to refrain from sin
    and love of the world

    B.   The people are urged to recall God's
    acts of mercy, past and future

        1.   God sent his son to rescue "us"
        from "the captivity of this age"

        2.   "Thrones and crowns" await those
        marked by the Name and the seal

        3.   God's people will be led in safety
        by the angels to "the city of God,"
        while sinners will be ruled by the
        powers of death

III   The end time will see "teachings which are not of God"

    A.   God's law will be abrogated and his covenant broken

    B.   The godly are not to be deceived

        1.   God himself instituted the fast

Sa^{3}4,17-6,16
Sa^{1}3,1-4,33
Ach 24,4-26,18

        2.   Fasting must be accompanied by holiness

        3.   Fasting is efficacious

        4.   Prayer must be free from doubt

    C.   Being "wise to the times" will render God's people invincible and fearless

IV   The king of the North will appear

    A.   He will be labelled "king of Assyria" and "unrighteous king"

    B.   He will wreak havoc in Egypt

V   "A king will arise in the West"

    A.   He will be called "the king of peace"

    B.   He will kill the "unrighteous king" and vent his anger on Egypt

    C.   By a ruse he will deceive the saints

Sa^{3}6,16-8,14

    D.   God will reveal the king's signs to the saints

        1.   He will be accompanied by two sons, one on either side of him

        2.   The son on the right will have a devilish appearance and forsake the name of God

    E.   The wicked son (on the right) will assassinate his father and assume supreme power

        1.   He will issue a decree that "the priests of the land and all the saints" be seized

2. Sanctuaries will be closed, homes expropriated and the young be led into captivity

3. Abominations will be offered and the usurper will exalt himself to heaven

---

Sa³8,14-13,4
Ach 27,1-32,14

4. Cities and people will be in a state of great distress

VI "Three kings will arise in Persia"

   A. They will settle the Jews of Egypt in Jerusalem

   B. Dissension in Jerusalem will signal the advent of the "lawless one"

   C. War will break out between the kings of Assyria and the kings of Persia

VII A king from "the city of the sun" will make his appearance

   A. He will kill the Assyrian kings in Memphis

   B. He will order the destruction of the heathen and their cults

   C. Sanctuaries will be rebuilt and the worship of God will be re-instituted

   D. A general state of prosperity and bliss will exist

VIII In the fourth year of the king of "the city of the sun" the lawless one will present himself

   A. He will claim to be the anointed one (christos)

   B. The saints are given the signs by which the true christos can be recognized

---

Sa³13,4-14,17
Sa¹5,1-6,20
Ach 32,15-34,17

   C. The lawless one will take his stand in "the holy place" and exercise power over all things except death

D. The signs of the lawless one will be revealed to the saints

E. Tabitha will hurry to Jerusalem to rebuke him for his acts

---

Sa^{3}14,17-16,8
Sa^{1}6,20-7,35

1. The lawless one will retaliate by pursuing her to the regions of the West, and cast her dead body on the temple

2. Tabitha will rise from the dead and renew her rebuke

F. Elijah and Enoch will come to oppose the lawless one

1. He will fight them "in the agora of the great city" for seven days

2. Elijah and Enoch will lie dead for three and a half days but renew their opposition on the fourth

---

Sa^{3}16,8-20,16
Sa^{1}7,35-13,11
Ach 35,1-40,16

3. The lawless one will again do battle against them but prove powerless

G. The lawless one will issue orders for the torture and persecution of the saints

1. Some will succumb to bribery, and receive diminished heavenly glory

2. Those who persevere will be seated on God's right hand

H. Sixty chosen righteous will don the armour of God and oppose the lawless one in Jerusalem

1. In retaliation he will order that "the righteous" be sacrificed

2. Many will recognize him from his acts as an impostor

I. Christos will send his sixty-four thousand angels to the assistance of the saints

    1.   Those with the Name and the seal
will be removed on angelic wings

    2.   Gabriel and Uriel will lead the
saints to "the holy land"

J.   The convulsions of nature will evoke
from the sinners a reproach against
the lawless one

Sa^3,20,16-20,23
Sa^{1}13,11-13,23

    1.   He will weep and bemoan his coming
doom

Sa^{1}13,23-14,29

    2.   He will order the death of the
saints

    3.   Sinners will weep and express their
impotence against the saints

    4.   The lawless one will join battle
with the saints, but angels will
come to their assistance

    5.   God will command fire from heaven
and earth to consume the sinners
and the devil

Sa^{1}14,29-14,33
Ach 41,1-41,3

K.   A "just judgement" will take place

(cf. Gk)
Ach 41,3-44,2

L.   Elijah and Enoch will annihilate the
lawless one and his adherents

IX Christos will make his appearance, accom-
panied by the saints

A.   The old earth will be destroyed

B.   Christos will create a new heaven and a
new earth

C.   The saints will share his company and
that of the angels for a thousand
years

4. Textual affiliation

It remains to investigate briefly the textual affiliation of our manuscript, and its value as a witness to the original text of the *Apocalypse of Elijah*. Several facts call for emphasis at the outset. In the first place, all our witnesses are fragmentary to a greater or lesser degree, and for that reason no *totally* accurate assessment can be made of their textual interrelationships. Secondly, it is beyond the scope of the present work to reconstruct a critical edition of the *Apocalypse of Elijah* – if indeed, such an undertaking were deemed possible in detail at our present state of knowledge about this work. We can at best give some pointers in what appears to be the right direction. Obviously not all of our extant witnesses are of the same textual value. In the third place, the enumeration of variant readings does contain an element of subjectivity, but the margin of variance is of no significant consequence for our purposes. Finally, though in what follows Sa^3 is the lemma text – and hence "lines of text" (etc.) refers to lines of Sa^3 – no value judgement is implied.

    a. Lines of text

        1) Sa^3 and Sa^2 share 47 lines of text

        2) Sa^3 and Sa^1 share 215 lines of text

        3) Sa^3 and Ach share 340 lines of text

    b. Number of variants

        1) Sa^2 versus Sa^3 = 9 = .19 variant per line

        2) Sa^1 versus Sa^3 = 115 = .53 variant per line

        3) Ach versus Sa^3 = 317 = .93 variant per line

From the above figures it is immediately clear that Sa^3 and Sa^2 are the most closely related and that Sa^3 and Ach are the farthest apart. But in order to get a more complete picture of the various interrelationships we need to pair off the manuscripts.

    a. Lines of text

        1) Sa^3 Sa^2 and Ach share 47 lines

        2) Sa^3 Sa^1 and Ach share 176 lines

        3) Sa^3 Ach and Sa^2 share 47 lines

        4) Sa^3 Ach and Sa^1 share 176 lines

        5) Sa^2 Ach and Sa^3 share 47 lines

        6) Sa^1 Ach and Sa^3 share 176 lines

    b. Number of variants

1) Sa^3 Sa^2 versus Ach = 36 = .77 variant per line

2) Sa^3 Sa^1 versus Ach = 98 = .56 variant per line

3) Sa^3 Ach versus Sa^2 = 1 = .02 variant per line

4) Sa^3 Ach versus Sa^1 = 40 = .23 variant per line

5) Sa^2 Ach versus Sa^3 = 5 = .11 variant per line

6) Sa^1 Ach versus Sa^3 = 30 = .17 variant per line

What has now further emerged is that Sa^2 is not only closely related
to Sa^3 but well-nigh consistently stands with the latter against Ach.
It is also clear that Sa^1, which unfortunately shares no text with
Sa^2, agrees much more frequently with Sa^3 than with Ach.

All the above are, of course, raw figures; that is to say, they
tell us nothing about the *kinds* of variant readings that unite or
divide manuscripts. Normally when one is dealing with texts as extensive as Sa^3 , Sa^1 and Ach, this fact poses no serious problem, since
matters average out. In the present situation we are, however, faced
with a complicating factor, which has the potential of wreaking havoc
with raw figures. Two (three) of our texts are written in Sahidic
but one in Achmimic, and the dialectical variations between these are
imprecisely known. Let us take one example to illustrate the problem
as we face it in the *Apocalypse of Elijah*. Six times in our Sahidic
witnesses we find 6ωΝΤ either as a verb or as a substantive, but in
only one case does Ach read the same word:

1,5 ΤΕΤΝ̄†6ωΝΤ	Sa^3 Sa^2: ΤΕΤΝ̄†ΝΟΥΚϹ̄	Ach (19,4)
4,1 Εϥ†6ωΝΤ	Sa^3: Αϥ†6ωΝΤ	Ach (23,4)
16,20 Εϥ6ωΝΤ	Sa^1: ϥΒωΛΚ	Ach (35,13)
17,4 ϥΝΑ6ωΝΤ	Sa^3 Sa^1: ϥΝΑΒω<Λ>Κ	Ach (36,1)
18,12 Ν̄ϥ6ΟΝΤ	Sa^3 = Sa^1: ϥΒωΛΚ	Ach (38,1)
19,9 ζΛΘΗ Π6ωΝΤ	Sa^3 = Sa^1: ζΙΤζΙ Ν̄ΤϥΒΛ̄ΚΕ Ach (39,7)

These variants and others of a similar kind have been included in
the *apparatus criticus,* but should they have been? One suspects that
at least 6ωΝΤ and ΒωΛΚ are nothing more than dialectical variations and hence of no more text-critical value than, for example,
the variation ΕΒΟΛ/ΛΒΛΛ , the likes of which have been excluded

from the *apparatus criticus*.[3] If, as is commonly held, the
Apocalypse of Elijah was first translated (from Greek) into Achmimic
and was from Achmimic rendered into Sahidic, one could argue that
the Sahidic translator would naturally render ⲃⲱⲁⲕ by ϭⲱⲛⲧ,
since the former is Achmimic and Subachmimic but apparently not
Sahidic (see Crum). But there would still remain the problem of
ⲛⲟⲩⲕⲧ̄, the nearest Sahidic equivalent of which is ⲛⲟⲩϭⲧ̄ , which we
might reasonably expect to find in our Sahidic texts - if Ach has
preserved the original Achmimic reading and if the development ran
from Achmimic to Sahidic. There is, therefore, good reason to attempt
to circumvent as much as possible the difficulties of dialectical
variation, and at the same time to try to go a step beyond a mere
enumeration of interrelationships. A computation of "additions" and
"omissions" will do the former, while an examination of some of the
"additions" and "omissions" ought to do the latter.

As before Sa^3 serves as our point of departure. Not included in
our statistics are additions and omissions of bound morphemes such as
articles and other prefixes, infixes or suffixes.

a.   Additions in Sa^2: total 0

b.   Omissions in Sa^2: total 4   = .085 per line
   1) Sa^2 versus Sa^3 = 0
   2) Sa^2 Ach versus Sa^3 = 4   = .085 per line

c.   Additions in Sa^1: total 11   = .051 per line
   1) Sa^1 versus Sa^3 = 5   = .023 per line
   2) Sa^1 versus Sa^3 Ach = 5   = .028 per line
   3) Sa^1 Ach versus Sa^3 = 1   = .006 per line

d.   Omissions in Sa^1: total 22   = .102 per line

---

[3]An interesting problem of a similar nature is ⲛ̄ϭⲓ/ϭⲉ. The former,
according to Crum, is both Sahidic and Achmimic, while the latter is
Achmimic but not Sahidic. In the *Apocalypse* we find ⲛ̄ϭⲓ in Sa^3
(and Sa^1) in 14 instances (1,10.18; 5,16; 9,1.10; 10,4.9.16.18.19;
14,9; 16,19; 17,3; 18,3) where Ach reads ϭⲉ, but in 6 cases (21,4.10;
22,9.15.17; 37,7) Ach reads ⲛ̄ϭⲓ in agreement with Sa^3 (in 37,7 Sa^3
has been reconstructed). Though we have not included these variants
in the apparatus, one might argue that they should have been.

1) Sa^1 versus Sa^3 = 8	= .037 per line	
2) Sa^1 versus Sa^3 Ach = 6	= .034 per line	
3) Sa^1 Ach versus Sa^3 = 8	= .045 per line	

e. Additions in Ach: total 44   = .129 per line

     1) Ach versus Sa^3 = 19   = .056 per line

     2) Ach versus Sa^3 Sa^2 = 5   = .106 per line

     3) Ach versus Sa^3 Sa^1 = 19   = .108 per line

     4) Ach Sa^2 versus Sa^3 = 0

     5) Ach Sa^1 versus Sa^3 = 2   = .011 per line

f. Omissions in Ach: total 76   = .223 per line

     1) Ach versus Sa^3 = 39   = .114 per line

     2) Ach versus Sa^3 Sa^2 = 7   = .149 per line

     3) Ach versus Sa^3 Sa^1 = 18   = .102 per line

     4) Ach Sa^2 versus Sa^3 = 4   = .085 per line

     5) Ach Sa^1 versus Sa^3 = 8   = .045 per line

The conclusions we reached earlier are confirmed by our further compu-
tations. The comparative figures for both additions and omissions in
Ach are more than twice as high as for Sa^1, a fact which shows that Ach
is indeed the farthest removed from Sa^3. When we look at the pairs
Sa^3 Sa^2 and Sa^3 Sa^1 in relation to Ach we notice that the figures are
again appreciably higher than for other combinations - something one
might likewise have expected on the basis of our previous findings.

When we examine in some detail the pluses and minuses in Ach it
becomes readily apparent that in both categories stylistic particles
play a prominent role. Thus we find, for example, that ⲁⲩⲱ is
"omitted" ten times (1,18 Sa^3 Sa^2 vs. Ach; 2,17 Sa^3 vs. Ach; 3,6 Sa^3
vs. Sa^2 Ach; 5,8 Sa^3 Sa^1 vs. Ach; 8,15 Sa^3 vs. Ach; 9,2 Sa^3 vs. Ach;
10,1 Sa^3 vs. Ach; 13,3 Sa^3 vs. Ach; 17,4 Sa^3 vs. Sa^1 Ach; 19,5 Sa^3
Sa^1 vs. Ach) and "added" three times (11,11 Sa^3 vs. Ach; 11,15 Sa^3 vs.
Ach; 17,17 Sa^3 Sa^1 vs. Ach). (ⲛ)ⲅⲁⲣ is omitted four times (1,8 Sa^3
Sa^2 vs. Ach; 1,22 Sa^3 vs. Sa^2 Ach; 4,12 Sa^3 vs. Ach; 18,18 Sa^3 vs. Sa^1
Ach) and added once (8,16 Sa^3 vs. Ach). ⲇⲉ is omitted twice (3,17
Sa^3 vs. Ach; 14,6 Sa^3 Sa^1 vs. Ach) and added twice (4,4 Sa^3 vs. Ach;
19,5 Sa^3 Sa^1 vs. Ach), though twice more in longer additions. ⲟⲩⲁⲉ
is omitted once (2,9 Sa^3 vs. Ach) but never added, except in a longer
addition. ⲭⲉ is omitted twice (3,10 Sa^3 Sa^2 vs. Ach; 20,5 Sa^3 Sa^1
vs. Ach) and added thrice (1,7 Sa^3 Sa^2 vs. Ach; 2,6 Sa^{3vid} vs. Ach;

5,14 Sa³ Sa¹ vs. Ach). ϭⲉ is omitted twice (2,18 Sa³ vs. Ach;
8,16 Sa³ vs. Ach) and added twice (1,18 Sa³ Sa² vs. Ach; 5,4 Sa³
Sa¹ vs. Ach). ⲁⲗⲗⲁ, ⲣⲱ and ⲉⲧⲓ are omitted thrice (3,19 Sa³ vs.
Ach; 12,10 Sa³ᵛⁱᵈ vs. Ach; 18,8 Sa³ vs. Sa¹ Ach) twice (4,14 Sa³
vs. Ach; 16,11 Sa³ Sa¹ vs. Ach) and once (2,11 Sa³ᵛⁱᵈ vs. Ach) respectively, but are never added. Similarly ⲉ₂ⲣⲁ̈ⲓ is omitted five
times (5,12 Sa³ vs. Ach; 10,2 Sa³ vs. Ach; 10,11 Sa³ vs. Ach; 17,8
Sa³ Sa¹ vs. Ach; 18,6 Sa³ vs. Ach), but is never added. On the other
hand, ⲁⲃⲁⲗ (ⲉⲃⲟⲗ) is added twice (6,8 Sa³ Sa¹ vs. Ach; 17,6 Sa³
Sa¹ vs. Ach), but never omitted.

As singular variants in Sa¹ we note that ⲁⲩⲱ is omitted once
(15,13) but is never added, and ⲣⲱ is added once (5,12) but never
omitted. Only in one occurrence of any of the particles on which we
have focused do Sa³ and Ach (possibly) line up against Sa¹: 16,9
ⲛ̄ⲧⲟⲕ Sa³ᵛⁱᵈ Ach: ⲡⲣ ϫⲉ Sa¹.

Perhaps more interesting and revealing than the presence or
absence of stylistic particles, when one attempts to assess the rela-
tive worth of the manuscripts, are the substantive pluses and minuses
we find upon a comparison of our witnesses. In Ach we have at least
seven sizable omissions which were caused by parablepsis:
1,3 ⲧⲉⲧⲛ̄ⲣ̄ⲛⲟⲃⲉ ⲁⲩⲱ Sa³ Sa² (om. ⲁⲩⲱ): om Ach. One suspects
that ⲁⲩⲱ is secondary and that, consequently, Sa² has preserved the
original text.
4,6-7 ⲧⲛⲏⲥⲧⲓⲁ ⲅⲁⲣ ⲉⲥⲟⲩⲁⲁⲃ Sa³: om Ach
9,6-7 ⲁⲗⲗⲁ ⲉⲣⲉⲡⲙⲟⲩ ⲡⲱⲧ ⲛ̄ⲧⲟⲟⲧⲟⲩ Sa³: om Ach
9,9-10 ₂ⲣⲁ̈ⲓ ₂ⲛ̄ ⲛⲉ₂ⲟⲟⲩ ⲟⲩⲟⲉⲓϣ ⲉⲧⲙ̄ⲙⲁⲩ Sa³: om Ach
11,17-18 ⲛ̄ⲥⲉϣⲗ ⲛ̄ⲡⲣ̄ⲡⲛⲟⲩⲉ ⲛ̄ⲛ₂ⲉⲑⲛⲟⲥ ⲛ̄ⲥⲉⲧⲁⲕⲟ ⲛ̄ⲛⲉⲩⲏⲏⲃ Sa³: om Ach
17,12 ⲉⲩϫⲱ ⲙ̄ⲙⲟⲥ ϫⲉ ϫⲓⲟⲣ Sa³ = Sa¹: om Ach
17,20-21 ⲛⲉⲛⲧⲁⲩ₂ⲩⲡⲟⲙⲓⲛⲉ ⲁⲉ Sa³: om Sa¹ Ach
Probably to be added is: 5,3 ⲁⲣⲓⲥⲁⲃⲉ ₂ⲛ̄ ⲡⲉⲟⲩⲟⲉⲓϣ Sa³ = Sa¹ᵛⁱᵈ: om
Ach.

In Sa³ there are two certain cases of sizable omissions caused by
parablepsis:
13,4 ⲛ̄ϥⲉⲓⲣⲉ Sa³: +ϥⲛⲁϫⲟⲟⲥ ⲙ̄ⲡⲟⲟ₂ ϫⲉ ⲉⲣⲓⲥⲛⲁϥ ϥⲉⲓⲣⲉ Ach. That a
reference to the moon has dropped out of the text of Sa³ is also clear
from ⲙⲛ̄ⲙⲁⲩ, which presupposes both sun and moon.
17,7 ϥⲛⲁⲉⲓⲛⲉ Sa³: ⲡⲣ ϥⲛⲁⲉⲓⲛⲉ ⲛ̄ⲛⲟⲩ₂ⲁⲁⲣⲉ ⲁⲃⲗ ₂ⲛ̄ ⲛⲟⲩⲁⲡⲏⲩⲉ Ach=

Sa¹. A third likely instance is: 11,4 ETⲘⲘⲀⲨ Sa³: + ⲀⲚ ⲚⲀⲞⲞⲨⲉ
ETⲘⲘⲞ Ach.

Sa¹ does not seem to have any singular cases of sizable omissions
by parablepsis. However, the omission of ⲀⲨⲰ ⲚⲀⲀⲰⲦⲂ ⲘⲘⲞⲞⲨ in 16,3
is a possible though not obvious instance.

From the above it is obvious that Ach has suffered more from
scribal parablepsis than has either of the other texts, and to that
extent reflects the least trustworthy tradition. In many cases the
resultant text of both Sa³ and Ach is intelligible, of course, but
this only enhanced parablepsis and does not argue against its having
occurred.

A brief survey of additions reveals that both Sa³ (and Sa¹) and
Ach contain evident expansions, though the latter somewhat more clearly
so than the former. In Ach we note the following:

1,2 Ⲭⲉ Sa³ Sa²: + ⲠϢⲎⲢⲉ ⲘⲠⲢⲰⲘⲉ Ach

1,10 ⲠⲬⲞⲉⲓ⳱ⲥ Sa³ Sa²: + ⲘⲠⲉⲀⲨ Ach. Cf. 1,18

1,22 ⲀⲢⲬⲎⲀⲅⲅⲉⲖⲞ⳱ⲥ Sa³ = Sa²: +ⲞⲨⲀⲉ ⲀⲀⲞⲨⲉ ⲚⲀⲢⲬⲎ Ach

2,13 ⲚⲦⲞⲞⲨ Sa³: + ⲤⲉⲚⲀⲬⲒ Ϣⲓⲡⲉ Ach

4,15 ⲉⲠⲠⲞⲀⲉⲘⲞ⳱ⲥ Sa³: + ⲀⲘⲉⲓⲀⲉ Ach

5,6 ⲠⲔⲀⲀ Sa³ Sa¹: ⲘⲚ ⲚⲉⲦⲀⲀⲢⲀϤ ⲘⲠⲔⲀⲀ Ach

5,16 ⲦⲞⲦⲉ Sa³ Sa¹: ⲠⲘⲞⲨ Ⲁⲉ ⲚⲀⲠⲰⲦ ⲀⲂⲀⲀ ⲘⲘⲀⲨ ⲀⲞⲨ Ach. Cf. 9,2.6

11,4 ⲬⲢⲎⲘⲀ Sa³: + ⲘⲠⲢⲠⲉⲉⲓ̈ⲉ ⲉⲦ- Ach

11,15 ⲘⲠⲔⲀⲀ Sa³: + Ⲁⲉ ⲘⲠⲉⲢ⳱ⲤⲎ⳱ⲥ Ach

12,6 Ⲭⲉ Sa³: pr ⲉⲨⳤⲞⲨ ⲘⲘⲀ⳱ⲥ Ach

12,9 ⲞⲨⲞⲚ Sa³ᵛⁱᵈ: Ⲁⲉ ⲠϢⲎⲢⲉ ⲚⲦⲀⲚⲞⲘⲓⲀ Ach

13,3 ⲀⲢⲓⲔⲀⲔⲉ Sa³: pr ϤⲚⲀⳤⲞⲞ⳱ⲥ Ⲭⲉ Ach

13,3 ⲀⲢⲓⲞⲨⲞⲉⲓⲚ Sa³: pr ϤⲚⲀⳤⲞⲞ⳱ⲥ Ⲭⲉ Ach

16,8 ⲚⲀⲦϢⲓⲡⲉ Sa³ Sa¹: + Ⲱ ⲠϢⲎⲢⲉ ⲚⲦⲀⲚⲞⲘⲓⲀ Ach

16,18 ⲚⳤⲀⲀⲉ Sa³ Sa¹: + ⲀⲠⲚⲞⲨⲦⲉ Ach

17,2-3 ⲉⲢⲉⲠⲔⲞ⳱ⲥⲘⲞ⳱ⲥ ⲦⲎⲢϤ ⲚⲀⲨ ⲉⲢⲞⲞⲨ Sa³ = Sa¹: ⲉⲠⲀⲀⲞ⳱ⲥ ⲦⲎⲢϤ ⲚⲞ
       ⲀⲢⲀⲨ ⲘⲚ ⲠⲔⲞ⳱ⲥⲘⲞ⳱ⲥ ⲦⲎⲢϤ Ach

17,23 ⲤⲉⲚⲀⳤⲢⲞ Sa³ᵛⁱᵈ Sa¹: pr ⲤⲉⲚⲀⲬⲒ ⲀⲘⲀⲦ Ⲁⳤ̄Ⲛ ⲀⲉⲚⲔⲉⲔⲉⲨⲉ Ach.
One must admit here, however, that an omission in Sa³ Sa¹ is also
quite possible.

18,8 ⲀⲀⲨ Sa³ Sa¹: +ⳤⲚ ⲚⲀⲀⲢⲠ Ach

18,13 ⲚⳤⲔⲉⲀⲉⲨⲉ Sa³ = Sa¹: + ⲀⲬⲉⲢⲞ ⲚⲀⲉⲚⲀⲎⲨⲉ Ach

20,1 ⲀⲨⲰ Sa³ᵛⁱᵈ: pr ⲠⲔⲀⲀ ⲚⲀϢⲞⲞⲨⲉ Sa¹ = Ach.

There is further the lengthy plus at 17,6 (see <u>app.crit.</u>) but due to a one line lacuna in Ach its full import cannot be determined.

In Sa^3 the following appear to be expansions:

2,1 ⲉⲃⲟⲗ ⲍⲛ̄ ⲧⲥⲁⲣⲝ Sa^{3vid}: om Sa^{2vid} Ach^{vid}

3,13 ⲉⲧϣⲟⲃⲉ Sa^3 Sa^{2vid}: om Ach

4,3 ⲙⲛ̄ⲛ̄ⲥⲱⲥ Sa^3: om Ach

4,10 ⲉⲩⲥ†ⲛⲟⲩϥⲉ Sa^3: om Ach. An omission in Ach is also a distinct possibility.

9,8 ⲉⲕⲱⲧⲉ ⲉⲍⲣⲁⲓ̈ Sa^3: om Ach

9,16-17 ⲉⲧⲛⲁϣⲱⲡⲉ Sa^3: om Ach

10,17 ⲛ̄ⲧⲉⲩⲛⲟⲩ Sa^3: om Ach

11,14-15 ⲛ̄ⲡⲉⲣⲥⲟⲥ ⲛⲁⲭⲓ Sa^3: ⲥⲉⲛⲁⲭⲓ Ach. As recorded above we find (virtually) the same plus in Ach but at a different point. It is difficult to know which of the two manuscripts, if indeed either, has preserved the original reading.

12,20 ⲛ̄ϭⲓ ⲡⲉⲭ̄ⲥ̄ Sa^{3vid}: om Ach

18,12 ⲛ̄ϭⲓ ⲡⲁⲧϣⲓⲛⲉ Sa^3 = Sa^1: om Ach

18,14 ⲉⲛϣⲏⲟⲩⲉ Sa^3 Sa^1: om Ach

19,12 ϣⲁⲛⲧⲟⲩⲭⲓⲧⲟⲩ Sa^3 = Sa^1: om Ach

19,16 ⲛ̄ⲥⲉⲛⲍⲕⲟ Sa^3 = Sa^1: om Ach^{vid}

20,8 ⲉⲩϣⲟⲩⲉⲓⲧ Sa^3 Sa^1: om Ach

20,12 ⲙⲛ̄ⲛⲟⲩⲑⲗⲓⲯⲓⲥ Sa^3 = Sa^1: om Ach

Singular pluses in Sa^1 are few:

15,12 ⲁⲛ Sa^3: + ⲛ̄ⲧⲟⲕ ⲉⲕⲧⲱϭⲉ ⲙ̄ⲙⲟⲕ ⲛ̄ⲉⲛⲉⲧⲟⲩⲁⲁⲃ Sa^1

18,19-20 ϥⲛⲁⲕⲱⲧⲉ ⲁⲛ ⲛ̄ⲥⲁ ⲛ̄- Sa^{3vid}: ⲙⲏ ⲉϥⲕⲱⲧⲉ ⲛ̄ⲧⲟϥ ⲉⲛ ⲛ̄ⲍⲟⲩⲟ ⲛ̄ⲥⲁ ⲛ̄- Sa^1

Though more variant readings could be cited, our overview has been sufficient to indicate the textual affiliation of Sa^3. Our survey suggests further that in Sa^3, and more generally in the Sahidic tradition, we are perhaps closer to the original text of the <u>Apocalypse of Elijah</u> than in the textual tradition represented by Ach.

COPTIC TEXT

and

TRANSLATION

[ⲁ̅]

ⲡ̄ϣⲁ·ϫⲉ· ⲙ̄[ⲡ̄ⲭ]ⲟ·ⲉⲓⲥ′ ⲁ[ϥϣⲱⲡⲉ ϣⲁⲣⲟⲓ
ⲉϥ·ϫⲱ· ⲙ̄·ⲙⲟⲥ· ⲛⲁ·ⲓ̈′ ϫⲉ· [ⲁϫⲓⲥ ⲙ̄ⲡⲉⲓ
ⲗⲁ·ⲟⲥ′ ϫⲉ·ⲧⲃⲉ· ⲟⲩ′ ⲧⲉ·ⲧ̄ⲛ̄[ⲣ̄] ⲛⲟ·ⲃⲉ ⲁ[ⲩⲱ
ⲧⲉ·ⲧ̄ⲛ̄·ⲟⲩ·ⲉϩ· ⲛⲟ·ⲃⲉ′ ⲉ·ⲭ̄ⲛ̄ ⲛⲉ·ⲧ̄ⲛ̄·ⲛⲟ·[ⲃⲉ
5 ⲉ·ⲧⲉ·ⲧ̄ⲛ̄·ⲧ̄· ϭⲱⲛⲧ· ⲙ̄·ⲡ̄ⲭⲟ·ⲉⲓⲥ′ ⲡⲛⲟⲩ·ⲧⲉ[
ⲡⲉⲛ·ⲧⲁϥ·ⲧⲁ·ⲙⲓ·ⲉ̣· ⲧⲏ·ⲩ̈·ⲧ̄ⲛ̄′ ⲙ̄·ⲡ̄ⲣ̄·ⲙⲉ·ⲣⲉ· ⲡⲕⲟ̣·ⲥ
ⲙⲟⲥ′ ⲟⲩ·ⲗⲉ· ⲛⲉ·ⲧ·ϣⲟ·ⲟⲡ· [ϩ]ⲙ̄ ⲡⲕⲟⲥ·ⲙⲟⲥ′ ⲛϣ[ⲟⲩ
ϣⲟⲩ· ⲅⲁⲣ· ⲙ̄·ⲡⲕⲟⲥ·ⲙⲟ̣[ⲥ]′ ⲡⲁ·ⲡⲁⲓ·ⲁ·ⲃⲟ·ⲗⲟⲥ′ ⲡⲉ̣[
ⲙⲛ̄· ⲛⲉϥ·ⲃⲱⲗ· ⲉ·ⲃⲟⲗ′ ⲁⲣⲓ· ⲡⲙⲉ·ⲉⲩ·ⲉ· ϫⲉ· ⲁϥ·ϣⲛ̄
10 ϩⲧ]ⲏϥ′ ϩⲁ·ⲣⲱ·ⲧ̄ⲛ̄′ ⲛ̄·ϭⲓ· ⲡ·ⲭⲟ·ⲉⲓⲥ′ ⲡⲉⲛ·ⲧⲁϥ·[ⲧⲁ
ⲙⲓⲉ ⲛ̄]·ⲕⲁ ⲛⲓⲙ′ ϫⲉ·ⲕⲁ·ⲁⲥ· ⲉ·ϥⲉ·ⲛⲁ2·ⲙ̄ⲛ̄· ⲉ·ⲃ[ⲟⲗ
ϩⲛ̄· ⲧⲉ·ⲭⲙⲁ·ⲗⲱ·ⲥⲓ·ⲁ′ ⲙ̄·[ⲡ]ⲁⲓ·ⲉⲓ·ⲁⲓ·ⲱⲛ′ ⲟⲩ·ⲙⲏ[ⲏ
ϣⲉ· ⲅⲁⲣ· ⲛ̄ⲥⲟⲡ· ⲁ·ⲡⲁⲓ·[ⲁ]ⲃ[ⲟ]ⲗⲟⲥ′ ⲉ·ⲡⲓ·ⲑⲩ·ⲙⲓ′ ⲉ·[ⲧ̄ⲙ
ⲕⲁ· ⲡⲣⲏ· ⲉ·ϣⲁ· ⲉ̣[ϩⲣ]ⲁ·ⲓ̈· ⲉ·ⲭ̄ⲙ̄· ⲡ[ⲕⲁϩ ⲟ]ⲩ·ⲗⲉ· ⲉ·ⲧ̄ⲙ·
15 ⲕⲁ· ⲡⲕⲁϩ· ⲉ·ϯ· [ⲕ]ⲁⲣ·ⲡⲟⲥ ⲉϥ·ⲟⲩ·ⲱ·ϣ·ϣ· ⲉ·ⲱⲙ̄ⲧⲕ
ⲛ̄·ⲛ̄ⲣ̄·ⲣⲱ·ⲙⲉ ⲛ̄·ⲑⲉ· ⲙ̄·ⲡⲉⲕⲣⲱⲙ· ⲉϥ·ⲡⲏⲧ· ϩⲛ̄· [ⲟⲩ
ⲣⲟ·ⲟⲩ·ⲉ′ ⲉϥ·ⲟⲩ·ⲱϣ· ⲉ·ⲟⲙ·ⲕⲟⲩ′ ⲛ̄·ⲑⲉ· ⲛ̄·ⲟⲩ·ⲙⲟ·ⲟⲩ[
ⲗⲩ·ⲱ· ⲉ·ⲧⲃ[ⲉ]· ⲡⲁ·ⲓ̈′ ⲁϥ·ϣⲛ̄·ϩⲧⲏϥ· ϩⲁ·ⲣⲟⲛ· ⲛ̄·ϭⲓ· ⲡⲛ̣[ⲟ
ⲧⲉ′ ⲙ̄·ⲡⲉ·ⲟⲟⲩ′ ϥⲛⲁ·ⲧ̄ⲛ̄·ⲛⲟ·ⲟⲩ· ⲙ̄·ⲡⲉϥ·ϣⲏ·ⲣⲉ· ⲉ[
20 ⲡⲕⲟⲥ·ⲙⲟⲥ′ ϫⲉ· ⲉ·ϥⲉ·ⲛⲁ2·ⲙ̄[ⲛ̄]· ⲉ·ⲃⲉⲗ′ ϩⲛ̄· ⲧⲁⲓ̣[
ⲭⲙⲁ·ⲗⲱ·ⲥⲓ·ⲁ′ ⲙ̄·ⲡⲉϥ·ⲧⲁ·ⲙⲉ· ⲁⲅ·ⲅⲉ·ⲗⲟ̣ⲥ̣[
ⲛ̄·ⲅⲁⲣ· ⲉϥ·ⲛⲏ·ⲩ· ϣⲁ·ⲣⲟⲛ′ ⲟ[ⲩ]·ⲗⲉ· ⲁⲣ·ⲭⲏ·ⲁ[ⲅⲅⲉ
ⲗⲟⲥ′ ⲁⲗ·ⲗⲁ· ⲁϥ·ϣⲃ̄[ⲧϥ]· ⲛ̄·ⲑⲉ· ⲛⲟⲩ·ⲣ[ⲱ
ⲙⲉ· ⲉϥ·[ⲛⲏⲩ ϣⲁ]·ⲣⲟ̣[ⲛ ϫⲉ· ⲉϥⲉⲛⲁ2ⲙ̄ⲛ̄

---

4 ⲟⲩ2 Sa³* | 14 ⲕⲁ – ⲉⲧⲙ Sa³ᶜ = Sa² Ach | 24 ⲉϥⲛⲏⲩ Sa³*ᵛⁱᵈ

2 ⲛⲁⲓ̈ Sa³ Sa²: om Ach | ϫⲉ Sa³ Sa²: + ⲛϣⲏⲣⲉ ⲙ̄ⲡⲣⲱⲙⲉ Ach | 3
ⲧⲉⲧ̄ⲛ̄ⲣ̄ ⲛⲟⲃⲉ Sa³ Sa²: om Ach | ⲁⲩⲱ Sa³: om Sa² Ach | 4 ⲉⲭ̄ⲛ̄ Sa³
Sa²: ⲁⲭⲉⲧⲛ̄ Ach | 5 ⲉⲧⲉⲧ̄ⲛ̄ϯ ϭⲱⲛⲧ Sa³ᵛⁱᵈ Sa² (ⲧⲉⲧ̄ⲛ̄-): ⲧⲉⲧ̄ⲛ̄ϯ
ⲕⲟⲩⲕⲧ̄ Ach | 6 ⲡⲉⲛⲧⲁϥⲧⲁⲙⲓⲉ ⲧⲏⲩ̈ⲧ̄ⲛ̄ Sa³ = Sa²: ⲉⲧⲁ2ⲧⲉⲛⲉ ⲧⲏⲛⲉ
Ach | 7 ⲛⲉⲧϣⲟⲟⲡ Sa³ Sa²: ⲛⲉⲧ- Ach | 7-8 ⲛϣⲟⲩϣⲟⲩ Sa³ Sa²:
pr ϫⲉ Ach | 10 ⲡⲭⲟⲉⲓⲥ Sa³ Sa²: + ⲙ̄ⲡⲉⲗⲩ Ach | 10-11
ⲡⲉⲛⲧⲁϥⲧⲁⲙⲓⲉ Sa³ᵛⁱᵈ Sa²ᵛⁱᵈ: ⲉⲧⲁ2ⲧⲁⲛⲟ Ach | 11 ⲛ̄ⲕⲁ Sa³ Sa²:
ⲛ̄2ⲱ Ach | ϫⲉⲕⲁⲗⲁⲥ Sa³ Sa²: ⲕⲁⲗⲁⲥ Ach | 12-13 ⲟⲩⲙⲛⲛϣⲉ Sa³ Sa²:
2ⲗ2 Ach | 14 ⲉϣⲁ Sa³: ⲁⲛⲡ̄ⲣ̄ⲣⲓⲉ Ach | ⲟⲩⲗⲉ Sa³ Sa²: ⲁⲟⲩ
Ach | 16 ⲙ̄ⲡⲉⲕⲣⲱⲙ Sa³ Sa²: ⲛ̄ⲟⲩⲕⲱ2ⲧ Ach | 16-17 ⲟⲩⲣⲟⲟⲩⲉ Sa³
Sa²: ⲟⲩ2ⲣⲁⲩ Ach | 18 ⲁⲩⲱ Sa³ Sa²: om Ach | ⲡⲁⲓ̈ Sa³ Sa²ᵛⁱᵈ:
+ ϭⲉ Ach | 19 ϥⲛⲁⲧ̄ⲛ̄ⲛⲟⲟⲩ Sa³: ⲁϥⲧ̄ⲛ̄ⲛⲁϥ Ach | 20 ϫⲉ Sa³ Sa²:
ⲕⲁⲗⲥ Ach | 22 ⲛ̄ⲅⲁⲣ Sa³: om Sa² Ach | ⲁⲣⲭⲏⲁⲅⲅⲉⲗⲟⲥ Sa³:
ⲁⲣⲭⲓⲁⲅⲅⲉⲗⲟⲥ Sa²: ⲁⲣⲭⲁⲅⲅⲉⲗⲟⲥ Ach | ⲁⲣⲭⲏⲁⲅⲅⲉⲗⲟⲥ Sa³ = Sa²: +
ⲟⲩⲗⲉ ⲗⲁⲟⲩⲉ ⲛ̄ⲁⲣⲭⲏ Ach | 24 ϫⲉ Sa³ⁱⁿᶜ: ⲕⲁⲗⲥ Ach |

[1]

The word of the Lord addressed me

as follows: "Say to this

people, 'Why do you sin and

multiply sin,

5   provoking to anger the Lord God

who made you? Do not love the

world nor what is in the world

for the world's pride and its destruction

are the devil's.'" Remember that the Lord

10   who created everything had compassion on you,

in order that he might rescue us from

the captivity of this age. For

often the devil has desired to

prevent the sun from rising over the earth and

15   to prevent the earth from giving produce, wishing

to devour men like fire racing through

straw, wishing to swallow them up like water.

And, because of this, the glorious God

had compassion on us. He will send his son to

20   the world in order that he might rescue us from the

captivity. For he did not inform angel

nor archangel when he came to us,

but he changed himself into a man,

when he came to us in order that he might rescue us

→   B̄

ⲉⲃⲟⲗ ϩⲛ̄ ⲧⲥ]ⲁⲣⳃ· ⲛ[ⲧⲉⲧⲛ̄ϣ]ⲱ·ⲡⲉ· ϭⲉ· ⲛⲁ̣[ϥ

· ·]ⲛ̄ϣⲏⲣ[ⲉ ⲉϥ]ϣⲱ·ⲡⲉ· ⲛⲏ·ⲧⲛ̄· ⲓ̈·ⲱⲧ· ⲁ·ⲣ[ⲓ ⲡⲙⲉ

ⲉⲩⲉ]· ϫⲉ· ⲁϥ·ⲥⲟⲃⲧⲉ· ⲛⲏⲧⲛ̄· ⲛ̄·ϩⲉⲛ·ⲑⲣⲟ·ⲛ[ⲟⲥ

ⲙ̄ⲛ̄· ϩⲉⲛ·ⲕⲗⲟⲙ′ ϩⲛ̄· ⲧⲡⲉ· ϫⲉ· ⲟⲩ·ⲟ·ⲛⲓⲙ′ ⲉ·ⲧ[ⲛⲁⲥⲱ

5 ⲧⲙ̄′ ⲛ̄·ⲥⲁ· ⲡⲉϥ·ϩⲣⲟ·ⲟⲩ′ ⲥⲉ·ⲛⲁ·ϫⲓ· ⲛ̄·ⲛⲉ·ⲑⲣⲟ·ⲛ[ⲟⲥ

ⲙ̄ⲛ̄· ⲛⲉ·ⲕⲗⲟⲙ′ ϩ[ⲛ̄]·ⲛⲉ·ⲧⲉ· ⲛⲟⲩ·ⲉⲓ· ⲛⲉ′ ⲡⲉ·ϫⲉ·

ⲡ̣[ϫⲟⲉⲓⲥ

†·ⲛⲁ·ⲥⲉ₂· ⲡⲁ·ⲣⲁⲛ′ ⲉ·ⲭⲛ̄· ⲧⲉⲩ·ⲧⲉ₂·ⲛⲉ′ ⲛ̄·ⲧ[ⲁⲥⲫⲣⲁ

ⲅⲓ·ⳃⲉ· ⲧⲉⲩ·ϭⲓϫ′ ⲛ̄ⲛⲟⲩ·ⲛⲓⲙ′ ⲥⲉ·ⲛⲁϩ·ⲕⲟ [ⲁⲛ

ⲟⲩ·ⲁⲉ· ⲛ̄·ⲥⲉ·ⲛⲁ·ⲉⲓ·ⲃⲉ· ⲁⲛ′ ⲟⲩ·ⲁⲉ· ⲙ̄·ⲡϣⲏ·ⲣ[ⲉ ⲛ̄

10 ⲧⲁ·ⲛⲟ·ⲙⲓ·ⲁ· ⲛⲁ·ϭⲛ̄·ϭⲟⲙ· ⲉ·ⲣⲟ·ⲟⲩⲁⲛ· ⲟⲩ·ⲁ̣[ⲉ ⲥⲉ

ⲛⲁ·ⲕⲱ·ⲗⲩ· ⲙ̄·ⲙⲟ̣ⲟⲩ· ⲁⲛ′ ⲛ̄·ϭⲓ· ⲛⲉ·ⲑⲣⲟ̣ⲥ̣· ⲉ·ⲧ[ⲓ

ⲁⲗ·ⲗⲁ· ⲥⲉ·ⲛⲁ·ⲙⲟ̣[ⲟ]·ϣⲉ· ⲙ̄[ⲛ̄]· ⲛ̄·ⲁⲅ·ⲅⲉ·ⲗⲟⲥ′

ϣⲁ· ⲧⲁ·ⲡⲟ·ⲗⲓⲥ [ⲛ̄]·ⲣⲉϥ·ⲣ̄· ⲛ̣[ⲟ]ⲃⲉ· ⲁⲉ· ⲛ̄·ⲧⲟ·ⲟⲩ′

ⲥⲉ·ⲛⲁ·ⲟⲩ·ⲉ·ⲧⲃ̄· ⲛⲉ·ⲑⲣⲟⲛⲟⲥ· ⲁⲛ· ⲉ·ϩⲣⲁ·ⲓ̈′ ⲁⲗ·ⲗⲁ̣· ⲥⲉ·

15 ⲛⲁ·ⲁ·ⲙⲁ₂·ⲧⲉ· ⲙ̄·ⲙⲟ·ⲟⲩ′ ⲛ̄·ⲥⲉ·ⲣ̄· [ⲭ]ⲟ·ⲉⲓⲥ′ ⲉ·ⲣⲟ·ⲟⲩ′

ⲛ̄·ϭⲓ· ⲛⲉ·ⲑⲣⲟ·ⲛⲟⲥ′ ⲙ̄·ⲡⲙⲟⲩ· ⲉⲃⲟⲗ· ϫⲉ ⲛ̄·ⲁⲅ·ⲅⲉ·

ⲗⲟⲥ′ ⲡⲓ·ⲑⲉ· ⲙ̄ⲛ̄·ⲙⲁ·ⲟⲩ· ⲁⲛ· ⲁⲩ·ⲱ· ⲁⲩ·ⲁ·ⲁⲩ· ⲛ̄·ϣⲙ̄·ⲙⲟ·[

ⲉ]·ⲛⲉϥ·ⲙⲁ· ⲛ̄·ϣⲱ·ⲡⲉ· ⲥⲱ·ⲧⲙ̄· ϭⲉ· ⲛ̄·ⲥⲁ·ⲃⲉ·ⲟⲩ· ⲛ̄·[

ⲧ]ⲉ̣· ⲡⲕⲁ₂′ ⲉ·ⲛ[.]·ⲧⲉ₂· ⲛⲉ·ⲡⲗⲁ·ⲟⲥ′ ⲉ·ⲧⲛⲁ·ⲁ·ϣⲁ·ⲓ̈[

20 ⲛ̄ⲧ]·ϩ̣ⲁ·ⲏ̣· ⲛ̄·[ⲛⲉⲟⲩ]·ⲟ̣·ⲉⲓϣ′ ϫⲉ· ⲉ̣ⲩ·[ⲛ]ⲁ·ⲕⲱ· ⲛⲁ·ⲟ̣ⲩ· ⲛ̄[

ϩⲉⲛⲥⲃⲟⲟⲩⲉ ⲉⲛⲁⲡⲛⲟⲩⲧⲉ ⲁ]ⲛ· ⲛⲉ′ ⲉⲩ[ⲛⲁ

---

5 ⲡⲉϥϩⲣⲟⲩ Sa³* | 9 ⲥⲉⲛⲁⲉⲓⲃⲉ Sa³* | 10 ⲉⲣⲟ Sa³* | 11 ⲙ̄ⲙⲟ
Sa³* | 12 ⲁⲁⲅⲉⲗⲟⲥ Sa³* | 14 ⲑⲣⲟⲥ Sa³* | 15 ⲙⲟⲟⲩ Sa³* |
17 ⲁⲩⲁⲩ Sa³* |

1 ⲉⲃⲟⲗ ϩⲛ̄ ⲧⲥⲁⲣⳃ Sa³ᵛⁱᵈ: om Sa²ᵛⁱᵈ Achᵛⁱᵈ | ⲛ̄ⲥⲁ ⲡⲉϥϩⲣⲟⲟⲩ Sa³:
ⲛ̄ⲥⲱⲓ̈ Ach | 6 ⲡϫⲟⲉⲓⲥ Sa³ᵛⁱᵈ: + ϫⲉ Ach | 7 †ⲛⲁⲥⲉ₂ ⲡⲁⲣⲁⲛ
Sa³: †ⲛⲁⲥⲉⲓ̈ ⲙ̄ⲡⲁⲣⲉⲛ Ach | 8 ⲧⲉⲩϭⲓⲝ Sa³: ⲛ̄ⲧⲟⲩϭⲓⲝ Ach | 9
ⲟⲩⲁⲉ Sa³: om Ach | 11 ⲉⲧⲓ Sa³ᵛⁱᵈ: om Ach | 13 ⲛ̄ⲧⲟⲟⲩ Sa³:
+ ⲥⲉⲛⲁϫⲓ ϣⲓⲡⲉ Ach | 17 ⲁⲩⲱ Sa³: om Ach | 18 ϭⲉ Sa³: om
Ach | ⲛ̄ⲥⲁⲃⲉⲟⲩ ⲛ̄ⲧⲉ Sa³: ⲛ̄ⲣⲙⲛ̄ϩⲏⲧ Ach | 19 ⲉ̣ⲛⲧⲉ₂ Sa³:
ⲉⲧⲃⲉ Sa² Ach | ⲛⲉⲡⲗⲁ<ⲛ>ⲟⲥ Sa³ = Ach: ⲛⲉⲉⲓⲡⲗⲁⲛⲟⲥ Sa² | 20
ⲛ̄ⲧϩⲁⲏ Sa³ᵛⁱᵈ: ⲛ̄ⲑⲁⲏ Sa²: ϩⲛ̄ ⲧϩⲁⲓ̈ Ach |

[2]

from the flesh, and that you might indeed become

his children (and) he your father. Remember

that he has prepared for you thrones

and crowns in heaven. For everyone who will

5   obey his voice will receive thrones

and crowns. "As for those who are mine," says the Lord,

"I will write my name upon their foreheads and set

a seal on their right hands." They will be neither hungry

nor thirsty, nor will the lawless

10   one prevail over them, nor will the

powers any longer hinder them;

but they will walk with the angels

to my city. Sinners, however,

will not outstrip the powers, but the powers

15   of death will seize them and have dominion

over them because the angels

do not obey them, and they have made themselves strangers

to his dwelling places. Hear now, you wise

of the earth, concerning the deceivers who will multiply

20   at the end time, because they will adopt

teachings which are not God's; they will

† ⲅ̄

ⲁⲑ]ⲉ·ⲧⲓ· ⲙ̄·ⲡⲛⲟ·ⲙⲟⲥ' ⲙ̄·ⲡⲛⲟⲩ·ⲧⲉ' ⲛⲁ̈ⲓ̈· ⲉⲧ̣[ⲉ
ⲡⲉ]ⲩ·ⲛⲟⲩ·ⲧⲉ· ⲡⲉ' ϩⲏ·ⲧⲟⲩ· ⟦ϩⲏ·ⲧⲟⲩ·⟧ ⲉⲩ·ϫⲱ· ⲙ̄·
ⲙ]ⲟⲥ· ϫⲉ· ⲛ̄·ⲧⲛⲉⲥ·ⲧⲓ·ⲁ· ϣⲟ·ⲟⲡ· ⲁⲛ· ⲟⲩ·ⲧⲉ·
ⲙ̄ⲡ]ⲉ·ⲡⲛⲟⲩ·ⲧⲉ· ⲥⲱⲛⲧ· ⲙ̄·ⲙⲟⲥ· ⲉⲩ·ⲉⲓ·ⲣⲉ· ⲙ̄·
ⲙ]ⲟ̣·ⲟⲩ· ⲛ̄·ϣⲙ̄·ⲙⲟ· ⲉⲧ·ⲁⲓ·ⲁ·ⲑⲏ·ⲕⲏ· ⲙ̄·ⲡⲛⲟⲩ·
ⲧ]ⲉ̣· ⲁⲩ·ⲱ· ⲉⲩ·ϥⲱ·ϭⲉ· ⲙ̄·ⲙⲟ·ⲟⲩ· ⲉ·ⲛⲉ·ⲣⲏⲧ'
ⲉⲧ]·ⲧⲁ·ⲓ̈·ⲏ·ⲟⲩ· ⲛⲁ·ⲓ̈· ⲉ·ⲧⲉ· ⲛ̄·ⲥⲉ·ⲥⲙ̄ⲙⲟⲛⲧ· ⲁⲛ'
ⲛⲟⲩ]ⲟ·ⲉⲓϣ· ⲛⲓⲙ' ϩⲛ̄· ⲧⲡⲓⲥ·ⲧⲓⲥ' ⲉⲧ·ⲧⲁ·ⲭ̄ⲣⲏ·ⲩ'
ⲙ̄ⲡ]ⲣ̄·ⲧⲣⲉⲩ·ⲡⲗⲁ·ⲛⲁ· ϭⲉ· ⲙ̄·ⲙⲱ·ⲧⲛ̄· ⲛ̄·ϭⲓ·
ⲛⲁ̈ⲓ]̈· ⲉ·ⲧⲙ̄·ⲙⲁⲩ' ⲁ·ⲣⲓ· ⲡⲙⲉ·ⲉⲩ·ⲉ' ϫⲉ· ⲁ·ⲡϫⲟ·ⲉⲓⲥ[
ⲥⲱ̣ⲛⲧ· ⲛ̄·ⲧⲛⲏⲥ·ⲧⲓ·ⲁ' ϫⲓⲛ· ⲧⲁϥ·ⲧⲁ·ⲙⲓ·ⲉ· ⲙ̄·ⲡⲏ·
ⲩⲉ' ⲉⲩ·ⲛⲟ·ϥⲣⲉ· ⲛ̄·ⲛ̄ⲣ·ⲣⲱ·ⲙⲉ' ⲉ·ⲧⲃⲉ· ⲙ̄·ⲡⲁ·ⲑⲟⲥ'
ⲙⲛ̄· ⲛⲉ·ⲡⲓ·ⲑⲩ·ⲙⲓ·ⲁ' ⲉ·ⲧϣⲟ·ⲃⲉ' ⲉⲧ·ϯ· ⲟⲩ·ⲃⲉ· ⲧⲏ·
ⲩ·ⲧⲛ̄· ϫⲉ·ⲕⲁ·ⲁⲥ' ⲉ·ⲛ·ⲛⲉ·ϥⲣ̄· ϩⲁⲗ· ⲙ̄·ⲙⲱ·ⲧⲛ̄'
ⲛ̄·ϭⲓ· ⲡⲟ·ⲛⲏ·ⲣⲟⲥ' ⲁⲗ·ⲗⲁ· ⲟⲩ·ⲛⲏ·ⲥⲧⲓ·ⲁ' ⲉ·ⲥⲟⲩ·ⲁ·ⲁⲃ̣[
ⲧⲉ·ⲛ̄·ⲧⲁϥ·ⲥⲱⲛⲧ· ⲙ̄·ⲙⲟⲥ' ⲡⲉ·ϫⲁϥ· ⲛ̄·ϭⲓ·
ⲡϫⲟ·ⲉⲓⲥ' ⲡⲉ·ⲧⲛⲏⲥ·ⲧⲉⲩ·ⲉ· ⲇⲉ· ⲉ̣ⲛ·ⲉϥ̄·ⲣ̄· [ⲛⲟ
ⲃⲉ· ⲛ̄·ⲟⲩ·ⲟ·ⲉⲓϣ· ⲛⲓⲙ· ⲉ·ⲟⲩⲛ· ⲕⲱϩ· ⲛ̄·ϩⲏ̣[ⲧϥ̄
ϩⲓ· ϯ·ⲧⲱⲛ' ⲁⲗ·ⲗⲁ· ⲡⲉ·ⲧⲟⲩ·ⲁ·ⲁⲃ' ⲙⲁ·ⲣⲉ̣[ϥⲛⲏ
ⲥ]ⲧⲉⲩ·ⲉ· ⲡⲉ·ⲧⲛ̣[ⲏ]·ⲥ̣ⲧⲉⲩ·ⲉ· ⲛ̄·ⲧⲉ· ⲉ·ⲛ̄[ϥⲟⲩⲁⲁⲃ

---

2 ϩⲏⲧⲟⲩ bis Sa^{3*} | 6 ⲙ̄ⲙⲟⲩ Sa^{3*} | 7 ⲥⲙⲟⲛⲧ Sa^{3*} | 10 ⲉⲧⲙ̄ⲙⲟⲩ Sa^{3*vid} | 15 ⲟⲛⲏⲥⲧⲓⲁ Sa^{3*}

1-2 ⲉⲧⲉ - ϩⲏⲧⲟⲩ Sa^{3} Sa^{2}: ⲧⲁⲩⲉⲓⲣⲉ ⲛ̄ⲧⲟⲩϩⲉⲓ ⲛ̄ⲧⲟⲩⲛⲉⲛⲉⲩ Ach | 3 ⲛ̄ⲧⲛⲏⲥⲧⲓⲁ Sa^{3}(-ⲛⲉⲥ-) Sa^{2}: ⲧⲛⲏⲥⲧⲓⲁ Ach | ⲟⲩⲧⲉ Sa^{3}: ⲟⲩⲇⲉ Sa^{2} Ach | 5 ⲛ̄ϣⲙ̄ⲙⲟ Sa^{3} Sa^{2}: ϣⲙ̄ⲙⲟ Ach | ⲙ̄ⲡⲛⲟⲩⲧⲉ Sa^{3} Sa^{2}: ⲙ̄ Ach | 6 ⲁⲩⲱ Sa^{3}: om Sa^{2vid} Ach | ⲉⲩϥⲱϭⲉ Sa^{3} Sa^{2}: ⲉⲩⲣ̄ ⲁⲡⲟⲥⲧⲉⲣⲉⲓ Ach | ⲉⲛⲉⲣⲏⲧ Sa^{3} = Sa^{2}: ⲛ̄ⲛ̄ϣⲡ ϣⲡ Ach | 7 ⲉⲧⲉ Sa^{3} Sa^{2}: ⲇⲉ Ach | ⲁⲛ Sa^{3} Sa^{2}: om Ach (but cf ⲥⲉⲥⲙⲁⲛⲧⲉ ⲛ̄ⲛⲟⲩⲇⲉⲓϣ) | 8 ⲧⲡⲓⲥⲧⲓⲥ Sa^{3} Sa^{2}: ⲡⲓⲥⲧⲓⲥ Ach | 10 ⲛⲁ̈ⲓ ⲉⲧⲙ̄ⲙⲁⲩ Sa^{3vid} Sa^{2}: ⲛⲉⲧⲙ̄ⲙⲟ Ach | ϫⲉ Sa^{3} Sa^{2}: om Ach | 11 ⲧⲛⲏⲥⲧⲓⲁ Sa^{3} Sa^{2}: ⲛⲏⲥⲧⲓⲁ Ach | ϫⲓⲛ ⲧⲁϥⲧⲁⲙⲓⲉ Sa^{3} Sa^{2}: ⲛ̄ⲧⲁϥⲧⲁⲛⲟ Ach | 13 ⲉⲧϣⲟⲃⲉ Sa^{3} = Sa^{2vid}: om Ach | 14 ⲉⲛⲛⲉϥⲣ̄ ϩⲁⲗ Sa^{3} Sa^{2vid}: ⲛⲉϥϣⲱⲃⲉ Ach | 15 ⲡⲟⲛⲏⲣⲟⲥ Sa^{3} Sa^{2vid}: ⲡⲡⲟⲣⲟⲥ Ach | 16 ⲛ̄ⲧⲁϥⲥⲱⲛⲧ Sa^{3}: ⲧⲉⲧⲁ̈ⲓⲥⲱⲛⲧ Ach | 17 ⲇⲉ Sa^{3}: om Ach | 17-18 ⲉⲛⲉϥⲣ̄ ⲛⲟⲃⲉ Sa^{3}: tr post ⲛⲓⲙ Ach | 18-19 ⲛ̄ϩⲏⲧϥ/ϩⲓ ϯⲧⲱⲛ Sa^{3}: tr Ach | 19 ⲁⲗⲗⲁ Sa^{3}: om Ach | 20 ⲛ̄ⲧⲉ Sa^{3}: ⲇⲉ Ach | ⲉⲛϥⲟⲩⲁⲁⲃ Sa^{3}: ⲉϥⲟⲩⲁⲁⲃⲉ ⲉⲛ Ach |

[3]

set aside God's law - people whose

god is their own belly, who say,

"Fasting has no validity, nor

did God institute it." (Thereby) they

5 estrange themselves from God's covenant

and deprive themselves of precious

promises; they are at no time

rooted in firm faith.

Do not let those people deceive

10 you. Remember that the Lord

instituted fasting from his creation

of the heavens, as a benefit to mankind on account of the passions

and the changing lusts which oppose

you, so that the evil one would not

15 deceive you. But holy fasting

is what he has instituted. The Lord

says, "He who fasts will never

sin, even though there be in him envy

and quarrelsomeness." But let him who is holy

20 fast. He who fasts, however, without being holy

ⲁ̅

ⲉ]ϥ̇ϯ˙ ϭⲱⲛ̅ⲧ˙ ⲛ̅˙ⲡⲭⲟ˙ⲉⲓⲥ˙ ⲙ̅ⲛ̇˙ ⲛⲉ̣[ⲕⲉ

ⲁⲅ˙ⲅⲉ˙ⲗⲟⲥ' ⲁⲩ˙ⲱ˙ ⲉ̣ϥ̇ϯ˙ ⲙ̅˙ⲕⲁ̣2˙ ⲛ̅˙ⲧⲉϥ˙ψ̣ⲩ̣[ⲭⲏ

ⲙ̅ⲛ̇˙ⲛ˙ⲥⲱⲥ˙ ⲉϥ˙ⲥⲱ˙ⲟⲩ2˙ ⲛⲁϥ˙ ⲉ˙2ⲟⲩⲛ˙ ⲛ̅˙[ⲟⲣⲅⲏ

ⲉ˙ⲡⲉ˙2ⲟ˙ⲟⲩ˙ ⲛ̅˙ⲧⲟⲣ˙ⲅⲏ' ⲟⲩ˙ⲛⲏ˙ⲥⲧⲓ˙ⲁ˙ ⲉ˙ⲥⲟⲩ˙ⲁ˙ⲁ[ⲃ

5 ⲛ̅˙ⲧⲁ˙ⲡⲭⲟ˙ⲉⲓⲥ' ⲥⲱⲛⲧ˙ ⲙ̅˙ⲙⲟⲥ' 2ⲛ̅˙ ⲟⲩ˙2ⲏ̣[ⲧ

ⲉϥ˙ⲟⲩ˙ⲁ˙ⲁⲃ' ⲙ̅ⲛ̇˙ 2ⲉⲛ˙ϭⲓⲭ' ⲉⲩ˙ⲟⲩ˙ⲁ˙ⲁⲃ' ⲧⲛⲏ[ⲥⲧⲓⲁ

ⲅⲁⲣ˙ ⲉ˙ⲥⲟⲩ˙ⲁ˙ⲁⲃ' ϣⲁⲥ˙ⲕⲁ˙ ⲛⲟ˙ⲃⲉ˙ ⲉ˙ⲃⲟⲗ˙ ϣ[ⲁⲥ

ⲑⲉ˙ⲣⲁ˙ⲡⲉⲩ˙ⲉ ⲛ̅˙2ⲉⲛ˙ϣⲱ˙ⲛⲉ' ϣⲁⲥ˙ⲛⲉϫ 2[ⲉⲛ

ⲁⲁⲓ˙ⲙⲟ˙ⲛⲓ˙ⲟⲛ' ⲉ˙ⲃⲟⲗ˙ ϣⲁ˙ⲥⲉ˙ⲛⲉⲣ˙ⲅⲓ' ϣⲁ ⲡ̣[ⲉⲣⲟ

10 ⲛⲟⲥ˙ ⲙ̅˙ⲡⲛⲟⲩ˙ⲧⲉ˙' ⲉⲩ˙ⲕ̅ⲛ̅˙ⲛⲉ˙ ⲉⲩ˙ⲥϯ˙ⲛⲟⲩ˙ϥ̣[ⲉ ⲉⲩ

ⲕⲁ˙ ⲛⲟ˙ⲃⲉ˙ ⲉ˙ⲃⲟⲗ' 2ⲛ̅˙ⲛ ⲟⲩ˙ⲡⲣⲟⲥ˙ⲉⲩ˙ⲭⲏ˙ ⲉ̣[ⲥ]ⲟⲩ˙

ⲁ˙ⲁⲃ˙ ⲛⲓⲙ˙ ⲅⲁⲣ' ⲛ̅˙2ⲏⲧ˙ ⲧⲏ˙ⲩ˙ⲧ̅ⲛ' ⲡⲉ˙ⲧⲛⲁ˙ⲃⲱⲕ'

ⲉ˙ⲃⲟⲗ˙ ⲉ˙ⲧⲥⲱ˙ϣⲉ˙ ⲛ̅ϥ˙ⲭⲓ˙ ⲉ˙ⲟ˙ⲟⲩ˙ 2ⲛ̅˙ ⲧⲉϥ˙ⲧⲉ˙ⲭⲛⲏ'

ⲉ˙ⲙ̅ⲛ̅˙ⲥⲟ˙ⲧ̅ⲃ̅ϥ' ⲣⲱ˙ ⲛ̅˙ⲧⲟ˙ⲟⲧϥ' ⲏ˙ ⲛⲓⲙ˙ ⲡⲉ˙ ⲉⲧ˙ⲛⲁ˙

15 ⲃⲱⲕ˙ ⲉ˙ⲃⲟⲗ' ⲉⲡ˙ⲡⲟ˙ⲗⲉ˙ⲙⲟⲥ' ⲉ˙ⲙ̅ⲛ̅˙ 2ⲱⲕ˙ 2ⲓ˙ⲱ˙ϣϥ˙

ⲉ˙ⲙⲏ˙ⲧⲓ˙ ⲉⲩ˙ϣⲁⲛ˙ϭⲛ̅ⲧϥ̅˙ ⲙⲏ˙ ⲥⲉ˙ⲛⲁ˙2ⲱ˙ⲧ̅ⲃ˙ ⲙ̅˙

ⲙⲟϥ˙ ⲁⲛ' ⲭⲉ˙ ⲁϥ˙ϣⲱⲥ˙ ⲛ̅˙ⲡⲟ˙ⲫⲓ˙ⲕⲓ˙ⲟⲛ' ⲛ̅˙ⲡ̅ⲣ̅˙ⲣⲟ'

ⲧⲁ˙ⲓ̈ 2ⲱ˙ϣϥ˙ ⲧⲉ˙ ⲧⲃⲉ˙ ⲉ˙ⲙ̅ⲛ̅˙ⲛ̅ϣ˙ϭⲟⲙ˙ ⲛ̅˙ⲗⲁ˙ⲗⲩ[

ⲉ]˙ ⲉⲓ˙ ⲉ˙2ⲟⲩⲛ' ⲉ˙ⲡ˙ⲙⲁ˙ ⲉ˙ⲧⲟⲩ˙ⲁ˙ⲁⲃ' ⲉϥ˙ⲟ˙ ⲛ̅˙2ⲏⲧ˙

ⲥⲛ[ⲁⲩ

20 ⲡ]ⲉ˙ⲧⲟ˙ ⲛ̅˙2ⲏⲧ˙ ⲥⲛⲁⲩ' 2ⲙ̅˙ ⲧⲉⲩ˙ⲡⲣⲟⲥ˙ⲉⲩ˙ⲭⲏ' [ⲉ

ϥⲟ] ⲛ̅˙ⲕⲁ˙ⲕⲉ˙ ⲉ˙ⲣⲟϥ˙ ⲁⲩ˙ⲱ˙ ⲛ̅ⲛ̣˙ⲕⲉ˙ⲁⲅ˙ⲅⲉ˙ⲗⲟ[ⲥ

---

2 ⲗⲱ Sa³ * | 13 ⲉⲧⲱϣⲉ Sa³ * | ⲉⲟⲩ Sa³* | 19 ⲉⲙⲁ Sa³*

3 ⲙⲛ̅ⲛ̅ⲥⲱⲥ Sa³: om Ach | 4 ⲟⲩⲛⲏⲥⲧⲓⲁ Sa³: ⲛⲏⲥⲧⲓⲁ ⲁⲉ Ach |
5 ⲛ̅ⲧⲁⲡⲭⲟⲉⲓⲥ ⲥⲱⲛⲧ Sa³: ⲧⲉⲧⲁⲓ̈ⲥⲱⲛⲧ Ach | 6 ⲉϥⲟⲩⲗⲁⲃ Sa³:
ⲟⲩⲗⲗⲃⲉ Ach | ⲉⲩⲟⲩⲗⲁⲃ Sa³: ⲟⲩⲗⲁⲃⲉ Ach | 6-7 ⲧⲛⲏⲥⲧⲓⲁ -
ⲉⲥⲟⲩⲗⲁⲃ Sa³: om Ach | 8-9 ϣⲁⲥⲛⲉϫ 2ⲉⲛⲁⲁⲓⲙⲟⲛⲓⲟⲛ Sa³:
2ⲁⲣⲉⲥϯⲕⲁⲁⲓⲙⲱⲛ Ach | 10 ⲉⲩⲥϯⲛⲟⲩϥⲉ Sa³: om Ach | 12 ⲅⲁⲣ Sa³:
om Ach | 13 ⲉⲧⲥⲱϣⲉ Sa³: ⲁⲧⲕⲁⲓ̈ Ach | 14 ⲣⲱ Sa³: om Ach |
15 ⲉⲡⲡⲟⲗⲉⲙⲟⲥ Sa³: + ⲁⲙⲉⲓ2ⲉ Ach | 16 ⲉⲙⲏⲧⲓ Sa³: ⲙⲏ Ach
| ⲙⲏ Sa³: om Ach | 16-17 ⲥⲉⲛⲁ2ⲱⲧ̅ⲃ̅ ⲙ̅ⲙⲟϥ Sa³ Sa^lvid:
ⲥⲉⲛⲁⲉⲁⲧ̅ⲃ̅ϥ̅ Ach | 17 ⲁⲛ Sa³ = Ach: ⲙ̅ⲙⲁⲩ Sa^lvid: ⲗⲁϥϣⲱⲥ Sa³
Ach: ⲗϥⲥⲱϣϥ Sa¹ | 18 ⲉⲙ̅ⲛ̅ⲛ̅ϣ6ⲟⲙ Sa³: ⲙ̅ⲛ̅ ϭⲟⲙ Sa¹ Ach | 20
2ⲙ̅ ⲧⲉⲩⲡⲣⲟⲥⲉⲩⲭⲏ Sa³: 2ⲛ̅ ⲧⲉϥⲡⲣⲟⲥⲉⲩⲭⲏ Sa¹: ⲧϥⲡⲣⲟⲥⲉⲩⲭⲏ Ach |
20-21 ⲉϥⲟ ⲛ̅ⲕⲁⲕⲉ Sa³ Sa^lvid: ⲉⲓ̈ⲉ ⲛ̅ⲕⲉⲓⲉ Ach^vid |

[4]

angers the Lord as well as the

angels, and he harms his own soul;

furthermore, he accumulates against himself wrath

for the day of wrath. Holy fasting

5   is what the Lord instituted with pure

intent and holy hands. For holy

fasting forgives sin,

heals diseases, casts out

demons, exerts power up to the

10   throne of God, as an ointment, as a fragrance,

as a remission of sin through holy prayer.

For who among you would go

out to the field, take pride in his skill

but fail to take a tool in his hand? Or who would

15   go to war without being equipped with armour?

If he be discovered, will he not be killed,

because he disregarded his duty toward the king?

In the same way, it is impossible for anyone

to enter the holy place in a state of doubt.

20   He who doubts in prayer

is darkness to himself, and the angels

ⲡⲓ]·ⲑⲉ· ⲉ·ⲣⲟϥ· ⲁⲛ′ ⲉ·ϣⲱ·ⲡⲉ· ϭⲉ· ⲛ̄·ⲧⲉ·ⲧⲛ̄ⲟ [ⲛ̄ⲟⲩ

ⲍ]ⲏⲧ· ⲛ̄·ⲟⲩ·ⲱⲧ′ ⲛ̄·ⲛⲟⲩ·ⲟ·ⲉⲓϣ· ⲛⲓⲙ′ ⲍⲙ̄· ⲡⲭⲟ[

ⲉⲓ]ⲥ′ ⲁ·ⲣⲓ· ⲥⲁ·ⲃⲉ· ⲍⲙ̄· ⲡⲉ·ⲟⲩ·ⲟ·ⲉⲓϣ′ ⲭⲉ· ⲉ·ⲧⲉ·ⲧⲛ̄′

ⲁ]ⲛⲟ·ⲉⲓ· ⲛ̄·ⲕⲁ· ⲛⲓⲙ′ ⲉ·ⲧⲃⲉ· ⲛⲉ·ⲣⲱ·ⲟⲩ· ⲛ̄·ⲛⲁⲥ·

5   ⲥ]ⲩ·ⲣⲓ·ⲟⲥ′ ⲙⲛ̄· ⲡⲃⲱⲗ· ⲉ·ⲃⲟⲗ′ ⲛ̄·ⲧⲡⲉ· ⲙⲛ̄· ⲡ̣

ⲕⲁ̣ⲍ′ ⲛⲉ·ⲧⲉ· ⲛⲟⲩ·ⲉⲓ· ⲛⲉ· ⲛ̄·ⲥⲉ·ϣ·ϭⲙ̄·ϭⲟⲙ·

ⲉⲣⲟ]·ⲟⲩ· ⲁⲛ′ ⲡⲉ·ⲭⲁϥ· ⲛ̄·ϭⲓ· ⲡⲭⲟ·ⲉⲓⲥ· ⲟⲩ·ⲁⲉ· ⲛ̄·

ⲥⲉ]ⲛⲁ·ⲣ̄· ⲍⲟ·ⲧⲉ· ⲁⲛ′ ⲍⲛ̄· ⲟⲩ·ⲡⲟ·ⲗⲉ·ⲙⲟⲥ′ ⲁⲩ·ⲱ[

ⲍⲟ]ⲧ̣ⲁⲛ· ⲉⲩ·ϣⲁⲛ·ⲛⲁⲩ· ⲉⲩ·ⲣ̄·ⲣⲟ· ⲉ·ⲁϥ·ⲧⲱ·ⲟⲩ·ⲛϥ̄ [

10   ⲍ]ⲙ̄· ⲡⲉ·ⲙⲍⲓⲧ′ ⲉⲩ·ⲛⲁ·ⲙⲟⲩ·ⲧⲉ· ⲉ·ⲣⲟϥ· ⲭⲉ· ⲡⲣ̄·ⲣⲟ· ⲛ̄·

ⲛ̣ⲁⲥ·ⲥⲩ·ⲣⲓ·ⲟⲥ′ ⲁⲩ·ⲱ· ⲡⲣ̄·ⲣⲟ· ⲛ̄·ⲧⲁ·ⲁⲓ·ⲕⲓ·ⲁ· ϥⲛⲁ·

ⲧ̣ⲁ·ϣⲟ· ⲛ̄·ⲛⲉϥ·ⲡⲟ·ⲗⲉ·ⲙⲟⲥ′ ⲉ·ⲍⲣⲁ·ⲓ̈· ⲉ·ⲭⲛ̄· ⲕⲏ·ⲙⲉ′

ⲙⲛ̄· ⲛⲉϣ·ⲧⲟⲣ·ⲧⲣ̄· ⲡⲕⲁⲍ· ⲛⲁ·ⲁ·ϣⲁ·ⲍⲟⲙ· ⲍⲓ· ⲟⲩ·

ⲥⲟⲡ′ ⲥⲉ·ⲛⲁ·ⲍⲁⲣ·ⲡⲁ·ⲭⲉ· ⲛ̄·ⲛⲉ·ⲧⲛ̄·ϣⲏ·ⲣⲉ· ⲟⲩⲛ̄·

15   ⲛ ⲟⲩ·ⲙⲛ̄·ϣⲉ· ⲛⲁ·ⲉ·ⲡⲓ·ⲑⲩ·ⲙⲓ· ⲉ·ⲡⲙⲟⲩ· ⲍⲛ̄· ⲛⲉ·

ⲍⲟ·ⲟⲩ· ⲉ·ⲧⲛ̄:ⲉⲙⲁⲩ· ⲧⲟ·ⲧⲉ· ϥⲛⲁ·ⲧⲱ·ⲟⲩⲛϥ̄ ⲛ̄·

ϭⲓ· ⲟⲩ·ⲣ̄·ⲣⲟ· ⲍⲙ̄· ⲡⲉ·ⲙⲛⲧ′ ⲉⲩ·ⲛⲁ·ⲙⲟⲩ·ⲧⲉ· ⲣⲟϥ′

ⲭⲉ· ⲡⲣ̄·ⲣⲟ· ⲛ̄·†·ⲣⲏ·ⲛⲏ· ϥⲛⲁ·ⲡⲱⲧ· ⲉ·ⲍⲣⲁⲓ̈· ⲉ·ⲭⲛ̄·

ⲑⲁ·ⲗⲁⲥ·ⲥⲁ· ⲛ̄·ⲑⲉ· ⲛ̄·ⲟⲩ·ⲙⲟⲩ·ⲉⲓ· ⲉϥ·ⲍⲙ̄·ⲍⲙ̄′

20   ϥⲛⲁ·ⲍⲱ·ⲧⲃ̄ ⲙ̄·ⲡⲣ̄·ⲣⲟ· ⲛ̄·ⲧⲁ·ⲁⲓ·ⲕⲓ·ⲁ· ⲥⲉ·ⲛⲁ·

ⲭⲓ· ⲙ̄·ⲡⲉ·ⲕⲃⲁ· ⲛ̄·ⲕⲏ·ⲙⲉ· ⲍⲛ̄· ⲟⲩ·ⲡⲟ·ⲗⲉ·ⲙⲟⲥ′

ⲙⲛ̄· ⲍⲉⲛ·ⲥⲛⲟϥ· ⲉⲩ·ⲟϣ· ⲥⲉ·ⲛⲁ·ϣ·ⲡⲉ· [

5 ⲉⲃⲟⲥ Sa³*vid | 12 ⲡⲟⲗⲟⲥ Sa³* | 16 ⲉⲧⲛ̄ⲙ(ⲁⲩ) Sa³*vid |
ⲛⲁⲧⲱⲟⲩⲛϥ̄ Sa³*

1 ⲉⲣⲟϥ Sa³ Sa¹: ⲛⲉⲙⲉϥ Ach | ⲉϣⲱⲡⲉ Sa³: ϣⲱⲡⲉ Sa¹ = Ach |
ⲛ̄ⲧⲉⲧⲛ̄ⲟ Sa³: ⲉⲧⲉⲧⲛ̄ⲟ Sa¹ = Ach | 3 ⲁⲣⲓⲥⲁⲃⲉ ⲍⲙ̄ ⲡⲉⲟⲩⲟⲉⲓϣ Sa³:
ⲉⲣ̄ⲣⲓ.ⲁⲕⲉ ⲍⲛ̄ ⲡⲉⲍⲣⲟⲉⲓ Sa¹: om Ach | 4 ⲛ̄ⲕⲁ Sa³: ⲛ̄ⲍⲱⲃ Sa¹:
ⲛ̄ⲍⲁⲧⲉ Ach | ⲛⲉⲣⲱⲟⲩ Sa³ = Sa¹: + ϭⲉ Ach | 4-5 ⲛ̄ⲛⲁⲥⲥⲩⲣⲓⲟⲥ Sa³:
ⲛ̄ⲁⲥⲥⲩⲣⲓⲟⲥ Sa¹ Ach | 6 ⲡⲕⲁⲍ Sa³ Sa¹: + ⲙⲛ̄ ⲛⲉⲧⲍⲁⲣⲁϥ ⲙ̄ⲡⲕⲁⲍ Ach
| ⲛⲉⲧⲉ ⲛⲟⲩⲉⲓ ⲛⲉ Sa³ Sa¹:†ⲛⲟⲩ ϭⲉ Ach | ⲛ̄ⲥⲉϣϭⲙ̄ Sa³: ⲥⲉⲛⲁϣϭⲙ
Sa¹ = Ach | 7 ⲡⲉⲭⲁϥ ⲛ̄ϭⲓ Sa³ Sa¹: ⲡⲁⲭⲉ Ach | 7-8 ⲛ̄ⲥⲉⲛⲁⲣ̄ ⲍⲟⲧⲉ
Sa³: ⲥⲉⲛⲁⲣ̄ ⲍⲟⲧⲉ Sa¹: ⲥⲉⲛⲁⲣ ⲍⲛ̄ⲱ²ⲉ Ach | 8 ⲍⲛ̄ ⲟⲩⲡⲟⲗⲉⲙⲟⲥ
Sa³ Sa¹: ⲍⲙ̄ ⲡⲡⲟⲗⲉⲙⲟⲥ Ach | ⲁⲩⲱ Sa³ Sa¹: om Ach | 9
ⲉⲗⲁϥⲧⲱⲟⲩⲛϥ̄ Sa³: ⲉϥⲧⲱⲛ Sa¹ = Achvid | 10-11 ⲛ̄ⲛⲁⲥⲥⲩⲣⲓⲟⲥ Sa³vid:
ⲛ̄ⲁⲥⲥⲩⲣⲓⲟⲥ Sa¹ | 12 ⲉⲍⲣⲁⲓ̈ ⲉⲭⲛ̄ Sa³: ⲍⲣⲁⲓ̈ ⲍⲓⲭⲛ̄ Sa¹: ⲁⲭⲛ̄ Ach
| ⲛⲉϣⲧⲟⲣⲧⲣ̄ Sa³: ⲛⲉϥϣⲧⲟⲣⲧⲣ̄ Sa¹ = Ach | ⲛⲁⲗⲱ ⲁⲍⲟⲙ Sa³:
ⲛⲁϣϩⲉⲍⲟⲙ Sa¹ = Ach | 14 ⲍⲓ ⲟⲩⲥⲟⲡ Sa³ Sa¹: + ⲭⲉ Ach | 15
ⲙⲛ̄ϣⲉ Sa³ (ⲙⲛ̄ϣⲉ) Sa¹: ⲍⲁⲍ Ach | 16 ⲧⲟⲧⲉ Sa³ Sa¹: ⲡⲙⲟⲩ ⲁⲉ
ⲛⲁⲡⲱⲧ ⲁⲃⲁⲗ ⲙ̄ⲙⲁⲩ ⲗⲟⲩ Ach | ϥⲛⲁⲧⲱⲟⲩⲛϥ̄ Sa³: ϥⲛⲁⲧⲱⲟⲩⲛ Sa¹ = Ach
| 17 ⲍⲙ̄ ⲡⲉⲙⲛⲧ Sa³ = Sa¹: ⲍⲛ̄ ⲛ̄ⲥⲁ ⲛ̄ⲡⲉⲙⲛ̄ⲧ Ach | 18 ϥⲛⲁⲡⲱⲧ Sa³
Ach: ϥⲡⲱⲧ Sa¹ | ⲉⲍⲣⲁⲓ̈ ⲉⲭⲛ̄ Sa³ Sa¹: ⲍⲓⲭⲛ̄ Ach | 20 ⲥⲉⲛⲁⲭⲓ Sa³:
ⲉϥⲛⲁⲭⲓ Sa¹: ϥⲛⲁⲭⲓ Ach | 21 ⲟⲩⲡⲟⲗⲉⲙⲟⲥ Sa³ Sa¹: ⲍⲉⲛⲡⲟⲗⲉⲙⲟⲥ Ach

[5]

do not obey him. If, however, you are

always single-minded in the Lord,

be wise to the times, in order that you may

discern all things regarding the kings of the

5   Assyrians and the destruction of heaven and

earth. "Those who belong to me will not be

overpowered," says the Lord, "nor will they

be afraid in battle." And

when they see a king who has arisen

10   in the north, they will name him the king of the

Assyrians and the unrighteous king. He will

increase his wars and disturbances

against Egypt. The land will groan

with one accord. Your children will be seized.

15   Many will long for death at that

time. Then a king will

arise in the west, whom they will name

the king of peace. He will run on

the sea like a roaring lion.

20   He will kill the unrighteous king.

Vengeance will be taken on Egypt by war

and there will be much bloodshed.

| 22   ⲉⲩⲟϣ Sa³ = Ach: ⲁⲩⲱ Sa¹ |

ⲋ̄

ⲍ̄ⲙ· ⲡⲉ·ⲍⲟ·ⲟⲩ· ⲉ·ⲧ̄ⲙ·ⲙⲁⲩ·ⲟⲩ· ϥⲛⲁ·ⲕⲉ·ⲗⲉⲩ·ⲉ· ⲛ̄[ⲟⲩⲉⲓ

ⲣⲏ·ⲛⲏ· ⲉ·ⲃⲟⲗ' ⲍ̄ⲛ· ⲕⲏ·ⲙⲉ' ⲙ̄ⲛ· ⲟⲩ·ⲁⲱ·ⲣⲉ·ⲗ ⲉ̣·[ⲥϭⲟⲩ

ⲉⲓⲧ' ϥⲛⲁ·ϯ· ⲛ̄·ⲟⲩ·ⲉⲓ·ⲣⲏ·ⲛⲏ' ⲛ̄·ⲛⲉ·ⲧ·[ⲟⲩⲁⲁⲃ

ϥⲛⲁ· ⲍⲓ·ⲧⲟ·ⲟⲧϥ· ⲛ̄ϥ·ϫⲟ·ⲟⲥ· ϫⲉ· ⲟⲩ·ⲁ· [ⲡⲉ ⲡⲣⲁⲛ

5   ⲙ̄·ⲡⲛⲟⲩ·ⲧⲉ' ϥⲛⲁ·ϯ· ⲛⲟⲩ·ⲉ·ⲟ·ⲟⲩ' ⲛ̄·ⲛ·ⲟⲩ·[ⲏⲏⲃ

ⲙ̄·ⲡⲛⲟⲩ·ⲧⲉ' ϥⲛⲁ·ⲭⲓ·ⲥⲉ· ⲛ̄·ⲙ̄·ⲙⲁ· ⲉ̣·[ⲧⲟⲩⲁⲁⲃ

ϥⲛⲁ·ϯ· ⲛ̄·ⲍⲉⲛ·ⲁⲱ·ⲣⲟⲛ·' ⲉⲩ·ϣⲟ̣[ⲩⲉⲓⲧ

ⲉ·ⲡⲏ·ⲉⲓ· ⲙ̄·ⲡⲛⲟⲩ·ⲧⲉ· ϥⲛⲁ·ⲕⲟ·ⲧϥ· ⲍ̄ⲛ· [ⲙ̄

ⲡⲟ·ⲗⲓⲥ· ⲛ̄·ⲕⲏ·ⲙⲉ· ⲍ̄ⲛ· ⲟⲩ·ⲕⲣⲟϥ· ⲉ·ⲙⲛ̣·[ⲟⲩⲉⲓ

10 ⲙⲉ· ϥⲛⲁ·ⲭⲓ· ⲏ·ⲡⲉ· ⲛ̄·ⲛ̄ⲙ·ⲙⲁ· ⲉ·ⲧⲟⲩ·ⲁ·[ⲁⲃ

ϥⲛⲁ·ϣⲓ· ⲛ̄·ⲛ̄ⲉⲓ·ⲁⲱ·ⲗⲟⲛ' ⲛ̄·ⲛ̄·ⲍⲉ·ⲑⲛⲟⲥ' ϥⲛⲁ·

ⲭⲓ· ⲏ·ⲡⲉ· ⲛ̄·ⲛⲉⲩ·ⲭⲣⲏ·ⲙⲁ' ϥⲛⲁ·ⲧⲁ·ⲍⲟ· ⲛ̄·ⲍⲉⲛ'

ⲟⲩ·ⲏ·ⲏⲃ' ⲉ·ⲣⲟ·ⲟⲩ· ϥⲛⲁ·ⲕⲉ·ⲗⲉⲩ·ⲉ· ⲛ̄·ⲥⲉ·ϭⲱ·[ⲡⲉ

ⲛ̄·ⲛ·ⲥⲁ·ⲃⲉ·ⲉⲩ· ⲙ̄·ⲡⲕⲁⲍ' ⲙ̄ⲛ· ⲛⲟϭ· ⲙ̄·ⲡ·[ⲗⲁ

15 ⲟⲥ' ⲛ̄·ⲥⲉ·ⲭⲓ·ⲧⲟⲩ· ⲉⲩ·ⲙⲏ·ⲧⲣⲟ·ⲡⲟ·ⲗⲓⲥ· ⲉ·ⲧ̣·[ⲍⲓ

ϫⲛ̄· ⲑⲁ·ⲗⲁⲥ·ⲥⲁ' ⲉϥ·ϫⲱ· ⲙ̄·ⲙⲟⲥ' ϫⲉ [ⲟⲩ

ⲗⲉ̣·ⲡⲉ· ⲛ̄·ⲟⲩ·ⲱⲧ· ⲧⲉ' ⲉ·ⲧⲉ·ⲧⲛ̄·ϣⲁⲛ·ϭ̣·[ⲱⲧⲙ

ⲗⲉ· ϫⲉ· ϯ·ⲣⲏ·ⲛⲏ· ⲧⲉ' ⲙ̄ⲛ· [ⲡ]ⲣⲁ·ϣⲉ· ϯ·ⲛ̣·[

. . . . . . ·]ⲅⲟⲩ·ⲓ̈· ⲛ̄·[. . .]ⲓϣ·ⲧⲉ· ⲉⲓⲥ·[

---

1 ⲍ̄ⲙ̄ ⲡⲉⲍⲟ Sa³ * | 7 ⲍⲉⲛⲁⲱⲣⲟⲛ Sa³ * |

1 ⲍ̄ⲙ̄ ⲡⲉⲍⲟⲟⲩ Sa³: ⲍ̄ⲛ̄ ⲛⲉⲍⲟⲟⲩⲉ Sa¹ = Ach (ⲛ̄ⲛⲍ-) | ⲉⲧⲙ̄ⲙⲁⲩⲟⲩ
Sa³: ⲉⲧⲙ̄ⲙⲁⲩ Sa¹ = Ach | ϥⲛⲁⲕⲉⲗⲉⲩⲉ Sa³ Sa¹: ⲁⲧⲁϥⲕ̄ⲕⲉⲗⲉⲩⲉ Ach
| 3 ⲟⲩⲉⲓⲣⲏⲛⲏ Sa³ Sa¹: ϯⲣⲏⲛⲏ Ach | ⲛ̄ⲛⲉⲧⲟⲩⲁⲁⲃ Sa³: ⲛ̄ⲛⲁⲉⲓ
ⲉⲧⲟⲩⲁⲁⲃ Sa¹ = Ach | 4 ϥⲛⲁⲍⲓⲧⲟⲟⲧϥ Sa³ = Sa¹: om Ach[vid] |
ⲛ̄ϥϫⲟⲟⲥ Sa³: ⲉϫⲟⲟⲥ Sa¹ | 5 ⲛⲟⲩⲉⲟⲟⲩ Sa³ Sa¹: ⲛ̄ⲍⲉⲛⲧⲁ·ⲓⲟ Ach |
ⲛ̄ⲛⲟⲩⲏⲏⲃ Sa³ = Sa¹: ⲛ̄ⲛⲉⲧⲟⲩⲁⲁⲃ Ach[vid] | 6 ϥⲛⲁⲭⲓⲥⲉ Sa³ Sa¹:
ⲟⲩⲭⲓⲥⲉ Ach | ⲙ̄ⲙⲁ Sa³ Sa¹: ⲛ̄ⲧⲟⲡⲟⲥ Ach | ⲉⲧⲟⲩⲁⲁⲃ Sa³[vid]
Sa¹: ⲛ̄ⲛⲉⲧⲟⲩⲁⲁⲃⲉ Ach | 7 ⲉⲩϣⲟⲩⲉⲓⲧ Sa³ Sa¹: tr post ⲙ̄ⲡⲛⲟⲩⲧⲉ
Ach | 8 ϥⲛⲁⲕⲟⲧϥ Sa³ Sa¹ (-ⲕⲧⲟϥ): + ⲗⲃⲁⲗ Ach | 11 ⲛ̄ⲛⲍⲉⲑⲛⲟⲥ
Sa³ Ach: ⲛ̄ⲍⲉⲑⲛⲟⲥ Sa¹ | 12-13 ⲛ̄ⲍⲉⲛⲟⲩⲏⲏⲃ Sa³[vid] = Ach: ⲛ̄ⲟⲩⲏⲏⲃ
Sa¹ | 13 ⲉⲣⲟⲟⲩ Sa³: ⲉⲣⲁⲧⲟⲩ Sa¹: ⲁⲣⲉⲧⲟⲩ ⲁⲣⲁⲩ Ach |
ⲛ̄ⲥⲉϭⲱⲡⲉ Sa³ Sa¹: ⲗϭⲱⲡⲉ Ach | 14 ⲛ̄ⲛⲥⲁⲃⲉⲉⲩ Sa³ Sa¹ (ⲛ̄ⲥⲁⲃⲉⲟⲩⲉ):
ⲛ̄ⲛ̄ⲣⲙ̄ⲛ̄ⲍⲏⲧ Ach | 15 ⲉⲩⲙⲏⲧⲣⲟⲡⲟⲗⲓⲥ Sa³: ⲁⲧⲙⲏⲧⲣⲟⲡⲟⲗⲓⲥ Sa¹ Ach
| 16 ⲉϥϫⲱ Sa³ Sa¹: ⲉⲩϫⲟⲩ Ach |

[6]

At that time he will decree

peace throughout Egypt and a worthless gift.

He will grant peace to the saints.

He will undertake to say, "The name of

5   God is one." He will bestow honor on the priests

of God. He will exalt the holy places.

He will give worthless gifts

to God's house. He will circulate among the

cities of Egypt by deceit, without their knowledge.

10   He will enumerate the holy places.

He will weigh the heathen idols. He will

count their wealth. He will appoint

priests for them. He will command that the wise

men of the land be seized along with the eminent ones of the

15   people, and that they be taken to a metropolis

by the sea, saying, "There is but one language."

But when you hear, "Peace and joy exist," I will

. . . .

↑   Z̄

ⲅⲁ]ⲣ· ⲉⲓⲥ· ⲛⲉϥ·ⲙⲁ·ⲉⲓⲛ· ϯ·ⲛⲁ·ϫⲟ·ⲟⲩ· ⲉ·ⲣⲱ·ⲧⲛ· [

ⲭ]ⲉ· ⲉⲧⲉ·ⲧⲛ·ⲁ·ⲥⲟⲩ·ⲱⲛϥ· ⲟⲩ·ⲛ̄·ⲧⲁϥ· ⲛ̄·ⲅⲁⲣ· ⲙ̄·ⲙⲁⲩ·

ⲛ̄·ϣⲏ·ⲣⲉ· ⲥⲛⲁⲩ· ⲟⲩ·ⲁ· ϩⲓ· ⲟⲩ·ⲛⲁⲙ· ⲙ̄·ⲙⲟϥ·

ⲁⲩ·ⲱ· ⲟⲩ·ⲁ· ϩⲓ· ⲃⲟⲩⲣ· ⲙ̄·ⲙⲟϥ· ⲡⲉⲧ·ϩⲓ· ⲟⲩ·ⲛⲁⲙ·

5 ⲁ]ⲉ· ⲙ̄·ⲙⲟϥ· ϥⲛⲁ·ϫⲓ· ⲛ̄·ⲛⲟⲩ·ϩⲟ· ⲛ̄·ⲇⲓ·ⲁ·ⲃⲟ·ⲗⲟⲥ·

ϥⲛⲁ·ϯ·ⲟⲩ·ⲉ· ⲡⲣⲁⲛ· ⲙ̄·ⲡⲛⲟⲩ·ⲧⲉ· ⲟⲩ·ⲛ̄ ϥ̄·ⲧⲟ·ⲟⲩ·

ⲅⲁⲣ· ⲛ̄·ⲣ̄·ⲣⲟ· ⲛⲏ·ⲩ· ⲉ·ⲃⲟⲗ· ϩⲙ̄· ⲡ̄ⲣ·ⲣⲟ· ⲉ·ⲧⲙ̄·

ⲙⲁⲩ· ϩⲣⲁ·ⲓ̈· ⲇⲉ· ϩⲛ̄· ⲧⲉϥ·ⲙⲁϩ·ⲙⲁ·ⲃⲉ· ⲛ̄·ⲣⲟⲙ·

ⲡⲉ· ϥⲛⲏ·ⲩ· ⲉ·ϩⲣⲁ·ⲓ̈· ⲉ·ⲙⲛ̄·ϥⲉ· ϥⲛⲁ·ⲕⲱⲧ· ⲛ̄·ⲛⲟⲩ·

10 ⲣ̄[ⲡ]ⲉ· ϩⲙ̄· ⲙⲛ̄·ϥⲉ· ϩⲙ̄· ⲡⲉ·ϩⲟ·ⲟⲩ· ⲉ·ⲧⲙ̄·ⲙⲁⲩ·

ϥ[ⲛ]ⲁ·ⲧⲱ·ⲟⲩ·ⲛ̄ϥ· ⲉ·ⲭⲱϥ· ⲛ̄·ϭⲓ· ⲡⲉϥ·ϣⲏ·ⲣⲉ·

ⲙ̄ⲙⲛ̄· ⲙ̄·ⲙⲟϥ· ⲛ̄ϥ·ϩⲱ·ⲧ̄ⲃ· ⲙ̄·ⲙⲟϥ· ⲡⲕⲁϩ·

ⲧⲏⲣ̄ϥ· ⲛⲁ·ϣⲧⲟⲣ·ⲧ̄ⲣ· ϩⲙ̄· ⲡⲉ·ϩⲟ·ⲟⲩ· ⲉ·ⲧⲙ̄·ⲙⲁ[ⲩ

ϥⲁ·ⲕⲉ·ⲗⲉⲩ·ⲉ· ⲛ̄·ⲛⲟⲩ·ⲇⲓ·ⲁ·ⲧⲁⲅⲙⲁ· ⲉ·ⲃⲟⲗ·

15 ϩⲓ·ⲭ̄ⲙ· ⲡⲕⲁϩ· ⲧⲏⲣ̄ϥ· ⲛ̄·ⲥⲉ·ϭⲱ·ⲡⲉ· ⲛ̄·ⲛⲟⲩ[

ⲏ·ⲏⲃ· ⲙ̄·ⲡⲕⲁϩ· ⲙⲛ̄· ⲛⲉ·ⲧⲟⲩ·ⲁ·ⲁⲃ· ⲧⲏ·ⲣⲟ[ⲩ

ⲉϥ·ϫⲱ· ⲙ̄·ⲙⲟⲥ· ϫⲉ· ⲁⲱ·ⲣⲉ·ⲁ· ⲛⲓⲙ· ⲉ[ⲛ

ⲧⲁ·ⲡⲁ·ⲓ̈·ⲱⲧ· ⲧⲁ·ⲁⲩ· ⲛⲏ·ⲧⲛ· ⲙⲛ̄· ⲛ̣[ⲁ

ⲅⲁ·ⲑⲟⲛ̣·

---

5 ⲛ̄ⲟⲩϩⲟ Sa³ * | 6 ⲙ̄ⲡⲛⲟⲩ Sa³ * | 9 ⲙⲛ̄ϥⲉ Sa³ * |

[7]

for here are his signs. I will tell them to you

in order that you may recognize him. For he has

two sons, one on his right

and one on his left. Now, the one on the right

5   will assume a diabolical appearance.

He will abandon the name of God. For

four kings come from that king.

And in his thirtieth year

when he comes to Memphis he will construct a

10   temple in Memphis at that time.

His own son will rebel against him

and kill him. The whole

land will tremble. At that time

he will issue a decree throughout

15   the entire land that the priests

of the land be seized along with all the saints,

saying, "Every gift which

my father gave you and all benefits

→ H̄

ⲧⲏ·ⲣⲟⲩ′ ⲧⲉ·ⲧⲛ̄·ⲛⲁ·ⲧⲁ·ⲗⲩ· ⲉⲩ·ⲕⲏⲃ′ ϥⲛ̣[ⲁ

ⲧⲁⲙ· ⲛ̄ⲛ̄ⲙ·ⲙⲁ· ⲉ·ⲧⲟⲩ·ⲁ·ⲁⲃ′ ϥⲛⲁ·ϥ̣ⲓ· ⲙ̄[ⲙⲁⲩ

ⲙ̄′′ⲡⲉⲩ·ⲏ·ⲉⲓ′′ ϥⲛⲁ·ⲗⲓ·ⲭⲙⲁ·ⲗⲱ·ⲧⲓ·ⲍⲉ [ⲛ̄

ⲛⲉⲩ·ϣⲏ·ⲣⲉ′ ⲉⲩ·ⲉ·ⲭⲙⲁ·ⲗⲱ·ⲥⲓ·ⲁ· ϥⲛⲁ[ⲕⲉ

5 ⲗⲉⲩ·ⲉ· ⲛ̄·ⲥⲉ·ⲉⲓ·ⲣⲉ· ⲛ̄·ⲍⲉⲛ·ⲑⲩ·ⲥⲓ·ⲁ′ ⲙⲛ̣· [ⲍⲉⲛ

ⲃⲟ·ⲧⲉ· ⲍⲓ·ⲝ̄ⲙ· ⲡⲕⲁⲍ′ ⲙⲛ̄· ⲍⲉⲛ·ⲥⲓ·ϣⲉ· ϥ[

ⲛⲁ·ⲟⲩ·ⲱⲛⲍ· ⲉ·ⲃⲟⲗ′ ⲍⲁ· ⲡⲣⲏ· ⲙⲛ̄· ⲡⲟ·ⲟⲍ′ ⲍ̄ⲙ[

ⲡⲉ·ⲍⲟ·ⲟⲩ′ ⲉ·ⲧ̄ⲙ·ⲙⲁⲩ′ ⲛ̄·ⲛⲟⲩ·ⲏ·ⲛⲃ· ⲙ̄·ⲡⲕⲁⲍ[

ⲥⲉ·ⲛⲁ·ⲡⲱⲍ· ⲛ̄·ⲛⲉⲩ·ⲍⲟ·ⲉⲓ·ⲧⲉ· ⲟⲩⲟ·ⲉⲓ· ⲛⲏ·ⲧⲛ̄[

10 ⲛ̄·ⲁⲣ·ⲭⲱⲛ· ⲛ̄·ⲕⲏ·ⲙⲉ· ⲍ̄ⲛ· ⲛⲉ·ⲍⲟ·ⲟⲩ· ⲉ[ⲧ]ⲙ̄·ⲙⲁⲩ′

ⲭⲉ· ⲁ·ⲡⲉ·ⲧⲛ̄·ⲍⲟ·ⲟⲩ· ⲟⲩ·ⲉⲓ·ⲛⲉ· ⲡⲭⲓⲛ·[ⲟ6]ⲛⲥ·

ⲛ̄·ⲛ̄·ⲍⲏ·ⲕⲉ· ⲛⲁ·ⲕⲟⲧϥ· ⲉ·ⲍⲣⲁ·ⲓ̈· ⲉ·ⲭⲱ·ⲧⲛ̣′

ⲁⲩ·ⲱ· ⲥⲉ·ⲛⲁ·ⲍⲁⲣ·ⲡⲁ·ⲍⲉ· ⲛ̄·ⲛⲉⲧⲛ̄·ϣⲏ·ⲣⲉ· ⲉⲩ·

ⲍⲁⲣ·ⲡⲁ·ⲅⲏ′ ⲙ̄·ⲡⲟ·ⲗⲓⲥ· ⲛ̄·ⲕⲏ·ⲙⲏ· ⲥⲉ·ⲛⲁ·ⲗ̣·

15 ϣⲁ·ⲍⲟⲙ· ⲍ̄ⲙ· ⲡⲉ·ⲍⲟ·ⲟⲩ· ⲉ·ⲧ̄ⲙ·ⲙⲁⲩ· ⲁⲩ·ⲱ[ ]

ⲥⲉ·ⲛⲁ·ⲥⲱ·ⲧ̄ⲙ· ⲁⲛ· ϭⲉ· ⲉ·ⲡⲉ·ⲍⲣⲟ·ⲟⲩ· ⲙ̄·ⲡⲉⲧ·

✝· ⲉ·ⲃⲟⲗ′ ⲙⲛ̄· ⲡⲉⲧ·ϣⲱ·ⲱⲡ′ ⲍ̄ⲛ· ⲛⲁ·ⲅⲟ·ⲣⲁ[

ⲛ̄ⲙ·ⲡⲟ·ⲗⲓⲥ′ ⲛ̄·ⲕⲏ·ⲙⲉ· ⲥⲉ·ⲛⲁ·ⲭⲓ· ϣⲟ·ⲉⲓϣ[

ⲥⲉⲛⲁⲣⲓ]ⲙ̣ⲉ· [ϭⲉ ⲍ]ⲓ ⲟⲩ·ⲥⲟⲡ′

1-2 ⲛ̄ⲙⲙⲁ Sa³* | 2 ⲉⲧⲟⲩⲁⲁⲃ Sa³* | 9 ⲟⲩⲁ Sa³* | 19 ⲍⲓⲥⲟⲡ Sa³*|

13-14 ⲉⲩⲍⲁⲣⲡⲁⲅⲏ Sa³: ⲍ̄ⲛ ⲟⲩⲧⲱⲣⲡ Ach | 14-15 ⲥⲉⲛⲁⲁϣⲁⲍⲟⲙ Sa³:
ⲛⲁϣϭⲉⲍⲁⲙ Ach | 15 ⲍ̄ⲙ ⲡⲉⲍⲟⲟⲩ Sa³: ⲍ̄ⲛ ⲛ̄ⲍⲟⲟⲩⲉ Ach | ⲁⲩⲱ
Sa³: om Ach | 16 ⲥⲉⲛⲁⲥⲱⲧ̄ⲙ Sa³: + ⲅⲁⲣ Ach | ϭⲉ Sa³: om Ach
| 17 ⲡⲉⲧϣⲟⲟⲡ Sa³: ⲡⲉⲧⲧⲁⲩ Ach | ⲍ̄ⲛ Sa³: om Ach | 18
ⲥⲉⲛⲁⲭⲓ Sa³: ⲛⲁⲭⲓ Ach |

[8]

you shall return two-fold." He will

close the holy places. He will seize

their homes. He will take

their sons into captivity. He will

5   command that they perform sacrifices,

abominations, and galling acts upon the land. He

will appear beneath the sun and the moon at

that time. As for the priests of the land -

they will tear their garments. Woe to you

10   at that time, rulers of Egypt,

because your day has passed! The violence

of the poor will turn against you

and they will seize your sons

as plunder. The cities of Egypt

15   will groan at that time, and

no more will be heard the voice

of buyer and seller in the markets

of the cities of Egypt. They will collect dust.

The inhabitants of Egypt will weep

↑   Θ̄

ⲛ̄ϭ]ⲓˑ ⲛⲉⲧˑϣⲟˑⲟⲡˑ ϩ̄ⲛ̄ˑ ⲕⲏˑⲙⲉˑ ⲥⲉˑⲛⲁˑⲉˑⲡⲓˑ

ⲑ]ⲩˑⲙⲓˑ ⲉˑⲡⲙⲟⲩ′ ⲁⲩˑⲱˑ ⲛ̄ˑⲧⲉˑⲙⲟⲩ′ ⲡⲱⲧ′

ⲛ̄]ˑⲥⲁˑⲃⲟⲗˑ ⲙ̄ⲙⲟˑⲟⲩ′ ⲥⲉˑⲛⲁˑⲃⲱⲕˑ ⲉˑⲭ̄ⲛ̄ˑ ⲛ̄ⲙˑ

ⲡⲉˑⲧⲣⲁ′ ⲛ̄ˑⲥⲉˑϥⲟˑϭⲟⲩ′ ⲉˑⲃⲟⲗ′ ϩⲓˑⲭⲱˑⲟⲩ′ ⲉⲩˑ

5 ⲭⲱˑ ⲙ̄ⲙⲟⲥ′ ⲭⲉˑ ϩⲉˑ ⲉˑϩⲣⲁˑⲓ̈ˑ ⲉˑⲭⲱⲛ′ ⲁⲩˑⲱˑ

ⲛ̄ˑⲥⲉˑⲧ̄ⲙ̄ˑⲙⲟⲩ′ ⲁⲗˑⲗⲁˑ ⲉˑⲣⲉˑ ⲡⲙⲟⲩˑ ⲡⲱⲧˑ

ⲛ̄ˑⲧⲟⲟˑⲧⲟⲩˑ ⲟⲩˑⲑⲗⲓˑⲯⲓⲥ′ ⲉⲥˑⲕⲏⲃ′ ⲉˑⲥⲟϣˑ

ⲉˑⲕⲱⲧⲉˑ ⲉˑϩⲣⲁˑⲓ̈ˑ ϩⲓˑⲭ̄ⲙ̄ˑ ⲡⲕⲁϩ′ ⲧⲏⲣϥ̄′

ϩ̄ⲛ̄ˑ ⲛⲉˑϩⲟˑⲟⲩˑ ⲉˑⲧ̄ⲙ̄ˑⲙⲁⲩˑ ϩⲣⲁˑⲓ̈ˑ ϩ̄ⲛ̄ˑ ⲛⲉˑϩⲟˑⲟⲩ′

10 ⲟⲩ[ⲟ]ⲉⲓϣˑ ⲉˑⲧ̄ⲙ̄ˑⲙⲁⲩˑ ϥⲛⲁˑⲕⲉˑⲗⲉⲩˑⲉ ⲛ̄ˑ

ϭ̄ⲓ ⲡ̄ⲣ̄ˑⲣⲟ′ ⲛ̄ˑⲥⲉˑϭⲱˑⲡⲉˑ ⲛ̄ˑⲥⲁ̣ⲓˑⲙⲉˑ ⲛⲓⲙ′

ⲉⲧˑϯˑ ⲉˑⲕⲓˑⲃⲉˑ ⲛ̄ˑⲥⲉˑⲛ̄ˑⲧⲟⲩˑ ⲛⲁϥ′ ⲉⲩˑⲙⲏⲣ′

ⲛ̄ˑⲥⲉˑϯˑ ⲕⲓˑⲃⲉˑ ⲛ̄ˑⲛⲉˑⲁⲣⲁˑⲕⲱⲛ′ ⲛ̄ˑⲥⲉˑ

ⲥⲟˑⲱⲛⲅ′ ⲛ̄ˑⲛⲉⲩˑⲥⲛⲱˑⲱϥ′ ⲉˑⲃⲟⲗ′ ϩ̄ⲛ̄ˑ ⲛⲉⲩ′

15 ⲕⲓˑⲃⲉˑ ⲛ̄ˑⲥⲉˑⲧⲁˑⲁⲩ′ ⲛ̄ˑⲕⲗⲟˑ ⲛ̄ˑⲥⲟˑⲧⲟ′ ⲉˑⲧⲃⲉˑ

ⲧⲁˑⲛⲁⲅˑⲕⲏˑ ⲛ̄ˑⲛ̄ⲙ̄ˑⲡⲟˑⲗⲉˑⲙⲟⲥ′ ⲉˑⲧⲛⲁˑⲗˑ

ϣϣˑⲡⲉ′ ϥⲛⲁˑⲕⲉˑⲗⲉⲩˑⲉ′ ⲛ̄ˑⲥⲉˑϭⲱˑⲡⲉˑ ⲛ̄ˑϣⲏˑ

ⲣ[ⲉ] ϣⲏⲙˑ ⲛⲓⲙ′ ⲭ̄ⲛ̄ˑ ⲙ̄ⲛ̄ⲧ̄ˑⲥⲛⲟˑⲟⲩⲥ′ ⲛ̄ˑⲣⲟⲙˑ[

ⲡ̣[ⲉ] ⲉˑⲡⲉˑⲥⲏⲧ′ ⲛ̄ˑⲥⲉˑⲧⲥⲁˑⲃⲟˑⲟⲩ′ ⲉˑⲛⲉⲭˑ [ⲥⲟⲧⲉ ⲉ

20 ⲧⲙ]ⲉˑⲥⲓˑⲱ′ ⲙ̄ˑⲡⲕⲁϩ̣ˑ ⲉˑ[ⲥ]ⲉ̣ˑⲣ̄′ ϩⲏ̄ˑⲃ̣[ⲉ]′ [ϩ̣]ⲛ̣̄

---

7 ⲟⲑⲗⲓⲯⲓⲥ Sa³* | ⲉⲟⲟϣ Sa³* | 9 ϩ̄ⲛ̄ ⲛⲉϩⲟⲩ Sa³* | 12 ⲛⲁⲩ Sa³ * | 17 ⲛ̄ⲥϭⲱⲡⲉ Sa³* |

2 ⲁⲩⲱ Sa³: om Ach | ⲛ̄ⲧⲉ ⲙⲟⲩ Sa³: ⲡⲙⲟⲩ Ach | 3 ⲛ̄ⲥⲁⲃⲟⲗ ⲙ̄ⲙⲟⲟⲩ Sa³: ϥⲕⲗⲟⲟⲩⲉ Ach | ⲥⲉⲛⲁⲃⲱⲕ Sa³: ϩ̄ⲛ̄ ⲛ̄ϩⲟⲟⲩⲉ ⲉⲧⲙ̄ⲙⲟ ⲥⲉⲛⲁⲡⲱⲧ Ach | ⲉⲭ̄ⲛ̄ ⲛ̄ⲙ- Sa³: ⲁϩⲣⲏⲓ̈ ⲁⲛ- Ach | 4 ⲛ̄ⲥⲉϥⲟϭⲟⲩ Sa³: ⲥⲉϥϭⲉ Ach | ϩⲓⲭⲱⲟⲩ Sa³: om Ach | 6 ⲛ̄ⲥⲉⲧⲙ̄ⲙⲟⲩ Sa³: ⲁⲛ ⲛⲟⲩⲙⲟⲩ Ach | 6-7 ⲁⲗⲗⲁ - ⲛ̄ⲧⲟⲟⲧⲟⲩ Sa³: om Ach | 7 ⲉⲥⲟϣ Sa³: ⲥⲛⲁⲗϣⲉⲓ̈ Ach | 8 ⲉⲕⲱⲧⲉ ⲉϩⲣⲁⲓ̈ Sa³: om Ach | 9-10 ϩⲣⲁⲓ̈ - ⲉⲧⲙ̄ⲙⲁⲩ Sa³: om Ach | 16 ⲡⲟⲗⲉⲙⲟⲥ Sa³: ⲡⲟⲗⲓⲥ Ach | 16-17 ⲉⲧⲛⲁϣⲱⲡⲉ Sa³: om Ach | 17 ϥⲛⲁⲕⲉⲗⲉⲩⲉ Sa³: + ⲁⲛ Ach | 17-18 ϣⲏⲣⲉ Sa³: ⲁⲓⲗⲟⲩ Ach | 19 ⲛ̄ⲥⲉⲧⲥⲁⲃⲟⲟⲩ ⲉⲛⲉⲭ Sa³: ⲥⲉⲧⲉⲟⲩⲉ ⲁⲧⲉⲃⲁⲩ ⲁϯⲕ̄ Ach | 20 ⲙ̄ⲡⲕⲁϩ Sa³: ⲉⲧϩⲓⲭ̄ⲙ̄ ⲡⲕⲁϩ Ach | ⲉⲥⲉ- Sa³: ⲛⲁ- Ach | ϩ̄ⲛ̄ ⲛ̄ⲛⲟⲩⲟⲉⲓϣ Sa³: om Ach |

[9]

with one accord. They will desire

death but death will flee

from them. They will climb onto

rocks and jump down on them, and

5   say, "Fall on us!" And

they will not die but death runs away

from them, while double affliction

again increases throughout the whole land

at that time. At that time

10   the king will command

that every nursing woman be seized

and be brought to him in fetters

and that they suckle dragons and

that their blood be sucked from their

15   breasts and made poisonous. Because

of the stress of wars which

will take place, he will command that every

boy, twelve years and under, be seized

and be taught to shoot arrows.

20   The midwife of the land will mourn

→
                                                   ‾
                                                   ɪ

N̄]ΝΟΥ·Ο·ΕΙϢ΄   ΑΥ·ω·   ΤΕ·ΤΑⲤ·ΜΙ·ⲤΕ΄   Ε·ⲤΕϥ[ɪ   ЇΑΤⲤ̄
Ε·ᶻⲢΑ·Ї΄   Ε·ΤΠΕ΄   ΕⲤ·ΧϢ΄   Ⲙ̄·ΜΟⲤ΄   ΧΕ·   Ε·ΤΒΕ·   ○[Υ   Ν̄Τ
Α·ᶻⲘ̄·ΜΟⲤ΄   Ε·Τω·ΒΕ΄   ΕΧ·ΠΕ·   ϢΗ·Ⲣ·Ε΄   Ε·ΠΚΑ[ᶻ
Ε·ⲤΕ·ⲢΑ·ϢΕ΄   Ν̄·ϬΙ·   ΤΑ·ϬⲢΗ·ΝΗ΄   Ⲙ̄Ν̄Τ·ΠΑⲢ·

5   ΘΕ·ΝΟⲤ΄   ΕⲤ·ΧϢ·   Ⲙ̄·ΜΟⲤ΄   ΧΕ·   ΠΕ·ΟΥ·Ο·ΕΙϢ·   ⲛ[Ε
Ε·ΤⲢΕ·ΝⲢΑ·ϢΕ΄   ΧΕ·   Ⲙ̄Ν̄·   ϢΗ·Ⲣ·Ε΄   ϢΟ·ΟΠ   ⲚΑⲚ·
ᶻ]!·Ⲭ̄Ⲙ·   ΠΚΑᶻ΄   ΑΛ·ΛΑ·   ΝΕΝ·ϢΗ·Ⲣ·Ε΄   ΕΥ·[ᶻ]Ν̣̄·   Ⲙ̄·
ΠΗ·ΟΥ·Ε΄   ᶻⲘ̄·   ΠΕ·ᶻΟ·ΟΥ·   Ε·Ⲧ̄Ⲙ·ΜΑΥ΄   ΕΥ[ΝΑ]·Τω·
ΟΥ·ΝΟΥ·   Ν̄·ϬΙ·   ϢΟΜΝΤ·   Ν̄·Ⲣ̄·ⲢΟ΄   ᶻⲘ̄·   ⲡⲉ̣ⲣ̣·ⲥ̣ⲓⲥ΄

10   ΕΥ·ΑΙ·ⲬΜΑ·Λω·ΤΙ·ΧΕ·   Ν̄·ΝΙ·ΟΥ·ΑΛ·Ї΄   Ε·Τϣο·ΟΠ΄
ᶻⲚ·   ΚΗΜΕ΄   Ν̄·ⲥ̣ⲉ·ΧΙ·ΤΟΥ΄   Ε·ᶻⲢΑ·Ї΄   Ε·ΘΙ·Ε·ⲣ̣ΟΥ·ⲤΑ·
ΛΗΜ΄   Ν̄ⲤΕ·Ϭωⲣ̄ⲃ̄·   Ⲙ̄·ΜΟⲤ΄   ⲚΑΥ·   Ν̄·ΚΕ·ⲤΟⲡ[
ΤΟ·ΤΕ·   Ε·ΤΕ·Ⲧ̄Ν̄·ϢΑⲚ·Ⲥω·Ⲧ̄Ⲙ΄   ΧΕ·   ⲡωⲣⲭ·   ⲡⲉ[
Ⲙ̄Ν̄·   ΤΑⲤ·ΦΑ·ΛΙ·Α΄   ᶻⲚ·   ΘΙ·Ε·ⲣΟΥ·ⲤΑⲗⲏⲙ΄   ⲡϣ[ᶻ

15   Ν̄·ΝΕ·Ⲧ̄Ν̄·ᶻΟ·ΕΙ·ΤΕ΄   Ν̄·ΝΟΥ·Η·ΗⲂ   Ⲙ̄·ΠΚΑᶻ[
ΧΕ·   ϥ΄ΝΑ·ωⲤ̄Κ·   ΑⲚ΄   Ε·Ⲙ̄·ΠϥΕΙ·   Ν̄·ϬΙ·   ⲡϣⲏⲣ̣ⲉ[
Ⲙ̄·ΠΤΑ·ΚΟ·   Ν̄·ΤΕΥ·ΝΟΥ·   ϥΝΑ·ΟΥ·ΟΝᶻϥ·   ⲉ̣·[ⲃΟ]Λ΄
Ν̄]Ϭⲓ·   ΠΑ·ⲚΟ̣ΜΟⲤ·   ᶻⲚ·   ΝΕ·ᶻΟ·ΟΥ·   Ε·Ⲧ̄Ⲙ·Ⲙⲁ̣[Υ]   ᶻⲚ[
Ν̄ΜΑ]·   ⲉ̣·[ΤΟΥΑΑⲂ]΄   ⲥ̣ⲉ·ΝΑ·ΠωΤ·   Ν̄·ϬΙ·   Ν[Ⲣ̄ⲢΟ

20   Ν̄Ⲙ̄ΠΕⲢⲤΗⲤ   ᶻⲚ   ΝΕ]ᶻΟ·ΟΥ·   Ε·Ⲧ̄Ⲙ·Ⲙ[ΑΥ

---

8 ⲡⲏⲩ Sa[3]* | 10 ⲉϥϣⲟⲟⲡ Sa[3]*vid | 12 Ⲛ̄ⲥⲉ6ⲱⲣⲃ Sa[3]* |

1 ⲁⲩⲱ Sa[3]: om Ach | ⲉⲥⲉϥ1 Їⲁⲧⲥ Sa[3]: ⲁⲥⲛⲁϥ1 ⲉⲉⲧⲥ Ach | 2
ⲉᶻⲣⲁ·ї Sa[3]: om Ach | 2-3 Ⲛ̄ⲧⲁᶻⲙ̄ⲙⲟⲥ Sa[3]vid: ⲁ·ï2ⲙⲉⲥ Ach | 5
ⲡⲉⲟⲩⲟⲉⲓⲱ Sa[3]: ⲡⲛ̄ⲟⲩⲁ·ïⲱ Ach | 7-8 ⲉⲩᶻⲛ̄ Sa[3]: ⲁⲛⲁⲛ ⲁⲩᶻⲟⲟⲡ
ᶻⲛ̄ Ach | 8 ᶻⲙ̄ ⲡⲉᶻⲟⲟⲩ Sa[3]: ᶻⲛ̄ ⲛ̄ᶻⲟⲟⲩⲉ Ach | 8-9
ⲉⲩⲛⲁⲧϣⲟⲩⲛⲟⲩ Sa[3]: ⲁⲩⲛⲁⲧⲱⲛⲉ Ach | 9 ᶻⲙ̄ ⲡⲉⲣⲥⲓⲥ Sa[3]: ᶻⲛ̄
Ⲙ̄ⲡⲉⲣⲥⲏⲥ Ach | 10 ⲉⲩⲁⲓⲭⲙⲁⲗⲱⲧⲓⲍⲉ Sa[3]: ⲥⲉⲣ̄ ⲁⲓⲭⲙⲁⲗⲱⲧⲓⲍⲉ Ach
| 11 ⲉᶻⲣⲁ·ï Sa[3]: om Ach | 12 ⲛⲁⲩ Ⲛ̄ⲕⲉⲥⲟⲡ Sa[3]: ⲥⲉⲟⲩⲱᶻ Ⲙ̄ⲙⲟ
Ach | 13-14 ⲡⲉ - ⲓⲉⲣⲟⲩⲥⲁⲗⲏⲙ Sa[3]: ⲡⲉⲧᶻⲛ ⲧᶻⲓⲉⲣⲟⲩⲥⲁⲗⲏⲙ Ach
| 16 ⲡϣⲏⲣⲉ Sa[3]: ϣⲏⲣⲉ Ach | 17 Ⲛ̄ⲧⲉⲩⲛⲟⲩ Sa[3]: om Ach |
ϥⲛⲁⲟⲩⲟⲛᶻϥ Sa[3]: ϥⲛⲁⲟⲩⲱⲛᶻ Ach | 20 ⲉⲧⲙ̄ⲙⲁⲩ Sa[3]: om Ach |

[10]

then, and she who has given birth will look

heavenward and say, "Why did

I sit on the birthstool to bring a child into the world?"

The barren one and the virgin will

5   rejoice and say, "It is time

for us to rejoice, because we have no

children on the earth; rather our children are

in heaven." At that time three kings

will arise in Persia

10   who will capture the Jews who are

in Egypt and bring them to Jerusalem

and settle it with them once again.

Then, if you should hear that there is dissension

and <no> security in Jerusalem, rend

15   your garments, you priests of the land,

because the destroyer will not be long

in coming. Straightway the lawless one

will make his appearance in the holy places,

at that time. The Persian kings

20   will withdraw at that time.

ⲓ̄ⲁ̄

→

. .]ⲣ̣[. . . . .]·ϩⲣⲓⲧʹ ⲙ̄ⲛ̄· ⲛ̣ⲉ·ⲣⲱ·ⲟⲩʹ ⲛ̄·ⲛⲁⲥ·ⲥⲩ·ⲣⲓ[
ⲟ]ⲥʹ ϥⲧⲟ·ⲟⲩ· ⲛ̄ⲣ̄·ⲣⲟ· ⲛ̄·ⲥⲉ·ⲡⲟ·ⲗⲉ·ⲙⲓ· ⲙ̄ⲛ̄· ϣⲟⲙⲧ[
ⲥ]ⲉ·ⲛⲁ·ⲣ̄· ϣⲟⲙ·ⲧⲉ· ⲛ̄·ⲣⲟⲙ·ⲡⲉʹ ϩ̄ⲙ̄· ⲡⲙⲁ· ⲉ·ⲧ̄ⲙ̄·ⲙⲁⲩ̣[
ϣⲁⲛ·ⲧⲟⲩ·ϥⲓ· ⲙ̄·ⲡⲉ·ⲭⲣⲏ·ⲙⲁʹ ϩ̄ⲙ̄· ⲡⲙⲁ· ⲉ·ⲧ̄ⲙ̄·ⲙⲁⲩʹ
ⲟⲩ·ⲛ ⲟⲩ·ⲥⲛⲟϥ· ⲛⲁ·ⲥⲱ[ⲕ] ϫ̄ⲛ̄· ⲕⲱⲥʹ ϣⲁ· ⲙ̄ⲛ̄·ϥⲉʹ
ⲡⲉⲓ·ⲉ·ⲣⲟ· ⲛ̄·ⲕⲏ·ⲙⲉ· ⲛⲁ·[ⲣ̄ ⲥ]ⲛⲟϥ· ⲛ̄·ⲥⲉ·ⲧ̄ⲙ̄·ϣⲥⲱ·
ⲛ̄]ϩⲏⲧϥ· ⲛ̄·ϣⲟⲙ[ⲧ ⲛ̄ϩ]ⲟ̣ⲟⲩʹ ⲟⲩⲟ·ⲉⲓ· ⲛ̄·ⲕⲏ·ⲙ[ⲉ
ⲙ̄ⲛ̄ ⲛ]ⲉⲧ·ϣⲟ̣·ⲟⲡ· ϩ̄[ⲛ̄ ⲕⲏ]ⲙⲉʹ ϩ̄ⲛ̄· ⲛⲉ·ϩⲟ·ⲟⲩʹ ⲉ·ⲧ̄ⲙ̄[ⲙ]ⲁⲩ[
ϥⲛ]ⲁ̣·ⲧⲱ·ⲟⲩ·ⲛ̣̄ϥ̄ʹ ⲛ̄[ϭⲓ ⲟ]ⲩⲣ̄·ⲣⲟ· ϩ̄ⲛ̄· ⲧⲡⲟ·ⲗⲓⲥʹ ⲉ·ⲧⲉϣⲁⲩ·
ⲙⲟⲩ]·ⲧⲉ· ⲉ·ⲣⲟⲥ· ϫⲉ· ⲧⲡ̣[ⲟⲗⲓⲥ] ⲙ̣̄·ⲡⲣⲏ· ϩ̄ⲛ̄· ⲛⲉ·ϩⲟ·ⲟⲩ·
ⲉ·ⲧ̄ⲙ̄·
ⲙ]ⲁⲩʹ ⲡⲕⲁϩ· ⲧⲏⲣϥ ⲛⲁ·ϣⲧⲟⲣ·ⲧ̄ⲣ̄ʹ ϥⲛⲁ·ⲡⲱⲧ· ⲉ·ϩⲣⲁ·ϊʹ
ⲉⲙ]ⲛ̄·ϥⲉ· ϩ̄ⲛ̄· ⲧⲙ·ⲉϩ·ⲥⲟ·ⲉ· ⲛ̄·ⲣⲟⲙ·ⲡⲉʹ ⲛ̄·ⲛ̄ⲣ̄·ⲣⲱ·ⲟⲩʹ ⲙ̄ⲛ̄·
ⲙ̄]ⲡⲉⲣ·ⲥ[ⲏ]ⲥʹ ϥⲛⲁ·ⲉⲓ·ⲣⲉʹ ⲛ̄·ⲟⲩ·ⲕⲣⲟϥʹ ϩ̄ⲙ̄· ⲙ̄ⲛ̄·ϥⲉʹ ϥⲛⲁ·
ϩ]ⲱ·ⲧ̄ⲃ̄· ⲛ̄·ⲛⲉ·ⲣⲱ·ⲟⲩʹ ⲛ̄·ⲛⲁⲥ·ⲥⲩ·ⲣⲓ·[ⲟⲥ]ʹ ⲙ̄·ⲡⲉⲣ·ⲥⲟⲥʹ[
ⲛ̣ⲁ·ϫⲓ· ⲙ̄·ⲡ̣ⲉ·ⲕⲃⲁ· ⲙ̄·ⲡⲕⲁϩʹ ϥⲛⲁ[ⲕⲉ]·ⲗⲉⲩ·ⲉ· ⲛ̄·ⲥⲉ[
ϩⲱ·ⲧ̄ⲃ̄· ⲛ̄·ϩⲉ·ⲑⲛⲟⲥʹ ⲧⲏ·ⲣⲟⲩʹ ⲙ̄ⲛ̄· ⲛ̄ⲛ̣[ⲁ]ⲛ̣ⲟ·ⲙⲟⲥʹ ϥⲛⲁ[
ⲕⲉ·ⲗⲉⲩ·ⲉ· ⲛ̄·ⲥⲉ·ϣⲱⲗ· ⲛ̄·ⲛ̄ⲣ̄·ⲡⲏ·ⲟⲩ[ⲉ] ⲛ̄·ⲛ̄·ϩⲉ·ⲑⲛⲟⲥ[
ⲛ̄·ⲥⲉ·ⲧⲁ·ⲕⲟ· ⲛ̄·ⲛⲉⲩ·ⲏ·ⲏⲃʹ ϥⲛ[ⲁⲕⲉⲗⲉ]ⲩ·ⲉ· ⲛ̄·ⲥⲉⲕ̣[ⲱⲧ
ⲛ̄·ⲛⲉⲣ·ⲡⲏ·ⲩⲉ· ⲛ̄·ⲛⲉ·ⲧⲟⲩ·ⲁ·ⲁ[ⲃ ϥⲛⲁϯ ⲛ̄]ϩⲉⲛ·ⲇⲱ·ⲣⲟ̣[ⲛ
ⲉⲩⲕⲏⲃʹ ⲉ·ⲡⲏ·ⲉⲓ· ⲙ̄·ⲡⲛⲟⲩ·ⲧⲉ̣ [ϥⲛⲁϫⲟⲟⲥ ϫⲉ ⲟⲩⲁ ⲡⲉ
ⲡⲣⲁⲛ· ⲙ̄·ⲡⲛⲟⲩ·ⲧⲉʹ ⲡⲕⲁϩ [ⲧⲏⲣ̄ϥ̄ ⲛⲁⲟⲩⲱϣⲧ ⲙ̄ⲡⲉⲣⲥⲏⲥ
ⲡ̣ⲕⲉ·ϣⲱϫⲡ· ⲇⲉ· [ⲉⲧⲉⲙ̄ⲡⲟⲩⲙⲟⲩ ϩⲁ ⲛ̄ⲡⲗⲏⲅⲏ
ⲥⲉⲛ]ⲁ̣·ϫⲟ·ⲟⲥʹ ϫ[ⲉ ⲟⲩⲣ̄ⲣⲟ ⲛ̄ⲇⲓⲕⲁⲓⲟⲥ ⲡⲉⲛⲧⲁⲡϫⲟⲉⲓⲥ

---

4 ϩ̄ⲙ̄ ⲙⲁ Sa^3 * | 10 ⲣⲟⲥ Sa^3 * | 18 ⲛⲉⲩⲏⲏⲃ Sa^3* |

1]ϩⲣⲓⲧ Sa^3: ⲁϩⲣⲏⲁⲣⲓⲧ Ach | 1-2 ⲛ̄ⲛⲁⲥⲥⲩⲣⲓⲟⲥ Sa^3: ⲛ̄ⲁⲥⲥⲩⲣⲓⲟⲥ Ach | 2 ⲛ̄ⲥⲉⲡⲟⲗⲉⲙⲓ Sa^3: ⲥⲉⲛⲁⲙⲓϩⲉ Ach | 4 ⲭⲣⲏⲙⲁ Sa^3: + ⲙ̄ⲡⲣ̄ⲡⲉⲉϊⲉ ⲉⲧ- Ach | ⲉⲧ̄ⲙ̄ⲙⲁⲩ Sa^3: + ϩⲛ̄ ⲛ̄ϩⲟⲟⲩⲉ ⲉⲧ̄ⲙ̄ⲙⲟ Ach | 8 ⲛⲉⲧϣⲟⲟⲡ ϩ̄ⲛ̄ ⲕⲏⲙⲉ Sa^3: ⲛⲉⲧⲛ̄ϩⲏⲧϥ Ach | 9 ϥⲛⲁⲧⲱⲟⲩⲛ̄ϥ̄ Sa^3: ϥⲛⲁⲧⲱⲛⲉ Ach | 10-11 ϩ̄ⲛ̄ ⲛⲉϩⲟⲟⲩ ⲉⲧ̄ⲙ̄ⲙⲁⲩ Sa^3: om Ach | 11 ⲡⲕⲁϩ Sa^3: pr ⲗⲟⲩ ⲧⲉ Ach | ⲛⲁϣⲧⲟⲣⲧ̄ⲣ̄ Sa^3: ϩⲧⲁⲣⲧⲣⲉ Ach | ϥⲛⲁⲡⲱⲧ Sa^3: ⲡⲱⲧ Ach | 12 ⲛ̄ⲛ̄ⲣⲣⲱⲟⲩ Sa^3: ⲛ̄ⲣⲁϊ Ach | 12-13 ⲙⲛ̄ ⲙ̄ⲡⲉⲣⲥⲏⲥ Sa^3: ⲙ̄ⲡⲉⲣⲥⲏⲥ Ach | 13 ϥⲛⲁⲉⲓⲣⲉ Sa^3: ⲛⲁⲉⲓⲣⲉ Ach | 13-14 ϥⲛⲁϩⲱⲧ̄ⲃ̄ Sa^3: ⲥⲉⲛⲁϩⲱⲧⲃⲉ Ach | 14 ⲛⲉⲣⲱⲟⲩ ⲛ̄ⲛⲁⲥⲥⲩⲣⲓⲟⲥ Sa^3: ⲡⲣ̄ⲣⲟ ⲛ̄ⲁⲥⲥⲩⲣⲓⲟⲥ Ach | 14-15 ⲙ̄ⲡⲉⲣⲥⲟⲥ ⲛⲁϫⲓ Sa^3: ⲥⲉⲛⲁϫⲓ Ach | 15 ⲙ̄ⲡⲕⲁϩ Sa^3: + ϭⲉ ⲙ̄ⲡⲉⲣⲥⲏⲥ Ach | ϥⲛⲁⲕⲉⲗⲉⲩⲉ Sa^3: ⲗⲟⲩ ⲥⲉ ⲕⲉⲗⲉⲩⲉ Ach | 15-16 ⲛ̄ⲥⲉϩⲱⲧ̄ⲃ̄ Sa^3: ⲁϩⲱⲧⲃⲉ Ach | 16 ⲛ̄ϩⲉⲑⲛⲟⲥ Sa^3: ⲛ̄ⲛ̄ϩⲉⲑⲛⲟⲥ Ach | ⲛ̄ⲛⲁⲛⲟⲙⲟⲥ Sa^3: ⲛ̄ⲁⲛⲟⲙⲟⲥ Ach | 16-17 ϥⲛⲁⲕⲉⲗⲉⲩⲉ Sa^3: ⲥⲉⲛⲁⲣ̄ ⲕⲉⲗⲉⲩⲉ Ach | 17-18 ⲛ̄ⲥⲉϣⲱⲗ – ϥⲛⲁⲕⲉⲗⲉⲩⲉ Sa^3: om Ach | 18 ⲛ̄ⲥⲉⲕⲱⲧ Sa^3: ⲁⲕⲱⲧ Ach | 19 ⲛ̄ⲛⲉⲧⲟⲩⲁⲁⲃ Sa^3:

[11]

. . . . with the kings of the Assyrians;

and four kings will do battle with three.

They will spend three years there,

until they have removed the wealth in that place.

5   Blood will flow from Qus to Memphis.

The river of Egypt will turn into blood so that no one can drink

from it for three days. Woe to Egypt and to

those in Egypt! At that time,

a king will arise in the city which is

10   called "the city of the sun." At that time

the whole land will tremble. He will hasten

to Memphis in the sixth year of the kings of

the Persians. He will lay an ambush in Memphis. He will

kill the Assyrian kings. The Persians

15   will take vengeance on the land. He will command that

all the heathen and lawless be killed. He will

command that the pagan temples be plundered

and their priests be annihilated. He will command that

the holy places of the saints be rebuilt. He will give double gifts

20   to the house of God. He will say, "The name

of God is one." The whole land will worship the Persian.

And the remnant, which did not die under the blows

will say, "A righteous king it is whom the Lord

ⲚⲈⲦⲞⲨⲀⲀⲂⲈ Ach | ϥⲚⲀϯ Sa³: ⲤⲈⲚⲀϯ Ach | 20 ϥⲚⲀⲬⲞⲞⲤ Sa³ⁱⁿᶜ:
ⲤⲈⲚⲀⲬⲞⲞⲤ Ach | 22 ⲱⲱⲭⲛ Sa³: ⲤⲈⲈⲚⲈ Ach | ⲀⲈ Sa³: om Ach |

—
1 B

ⲧⲛ·ⲛⲟ·ⲟⲩϥ·   ⲛⲁⲛ′   ϫⲉ·   ⲛ̅[ⲛⲉ]ⲡⲕⲁ₂·   ⲣ̅·   ϫ[ⲁⲉⲓⲉ   ϥⲛⲁ

ⲕⲉ·ⲗⲉⲩ·ⲉ·   ϫⲉ·   ⲛⲉⲩ·†   ⲁⲗ·ⲗⲁⲩ·ⲉ′   ⲛ̅ⲣ̅·ⲣⲟ   [ⲛ̅]ⲱⲟ[ⲙⲧⲉ

ⲛ̅·ⲣⲟⲙ·ⲡⲉ′   ⲙ̅ⲛ·   ⲥⲟ·ⲟⲩ·   ⲛ̅·ⲛⲉ·ⲃⲟⲧ′   ⲡⲕⲁ₂·   ⲛ[ⲁ

ⲙⲟⲩ₂·   ⲛⲁ·ⲅⲁ·ⲑⲟⲛ′   ⲍ̅ⲛ·   ⲟⲩ·₂ⲉ·ⲛⲟⲩ·ϥⲉ·   ⲉ·ⲛⲁ[ϣⲱϥ

5 ⲛⲉ·ⲧⲟⲛ̅₂′   ⲛⲁ·.ⲃⲱⲕ·   ₂ⲁ·ϫⲱ·ⲟⲩ′   ⲛ̅·ⲛⲉ·ⲧⲙ̣[

ⲟⲩⲧ′   ϫⲉ·   ⲧⲟⲩⲛ·   ⲧⲏ̣[ⲩ]ⲧ̅ⲛ′   ⲉ·₂ⲣⲁ·ⲓ·′   ⲛ̅·ⲧⲉ·ⲧ̅ⲛ·6ⲱ[

ⲛⲙ̅·ⲙⲁⲛ′   ₂ⲙ̅·   ⲡⲉ̣[ⲓ]ⲙ̅·ⲧⲟⲛ′   ₂ⲣⲁ·ⲓ·   ⲛ̅·ⲧⲉ·   ₂ⲧ̅ⲛ   ⲧ

ⲙⲁ̣₂·ϥⲧⲟ·   ⲛ̅ⲣⲟⲙ·ⲡ[ⲉ   ⲙ̅ⲡⲣ̅]ⲣⲟ·   ⲉ·ⲧⲙ̅·ⲙⲁ[ⲩ

ϥ]ⲛⲁ·ⲟⲩ·ⲟⲛ₂·   ⲉ·ⲃⲟⲗ·   ⲟ[ⲩⲟⲛ   ⲉϥ]·ϫⲱ·   ⲙ̅·ⲙⲟ[ⲥ   ϫⲉ

10 ⲁ·ⲛⲟⲕ·   ⲡⲉ·   ⲡⲉ·ⲭ̅ⲥ̅   [ⲁⲗⲗ]ⲁ̣·   ⲛ̅ⲧⲟϥ·   ⲁⲛ·   [ⲡⲉ   ⲙ̅

ⲡⲣ̅·ⲡⲓ·ⲥⲧⲉⲩ·ⲉ·   ⲉ·ⲣⲟϥ·   [ⲉ]ϥϣ̣ⲁⲛ·ⲉⲓ·   ⲁⲉ·   ⲉϥⲛ̣[ⲏⲩ

ⲛ̅·6ⲓ·   ⲡⲉ·ⲭ̅ⲥ̅·   ⲉϥ·ⲛⲏ·ⲩ·   ⲛ̅ⲑⲉ·   ⲛ̅·ⲛⲟⲩ·ⲙⲉ·₂[

ⲁⲗ′   ⲛ̅·6ⲣⲟ·ⲟⲙ·ⲡⲉ·   ⲉ·ⲣⲉ·   ⲡⲉϥ·ⲕⲗⲟⲙ·   [ⲛ̅

6ⲣⲟ·ⲟⲙ·[ⲡ]ⲉ̣′   ⲕⲱ·ⲧⲉ·   ⲉ·ⲣⲟϥ·   ⲉϥ·ⲙⲟ̣·ⲟ̣·ϣⲉ[

15 ₂ⲓ·ϫ̅ⲛ·   ⲛ̅[ⲕ]ⲏ·ⲡⲉ′   ⲛ̅·ⲧⲡⲉ·   ⲉ·ⲣⲉ·   ⲙ̣ⲙⲁ·ⲉⲓ[ⲛ

ⲙ̅·ⲡⲉⲥ·[ⲧⲁ]ⲩ·ⲣⲟⲥ′   ⲥⲱⲕ·   ₂ⲁ·   ⲧⲉϥ·₂ⲏ[

ⲉ·ⲣⲉ·   ⲡⲕ[ⲟⲥ]ⲙⲟⲥ′   ⲧⲏⲣϥ̅′   ⲛⲁⲩ·   ⲉ·ⲣⲟϥ·   ⲛ̅·ⲑⲉ[ⲉ

ⲙ̅·ⲡⲣⲏ·   ⲉ̣[ⲧⲣ̅]·   ⲟⲩ·ⲟ·ⲉⲓⲛ·   ₂ⲛ̅·   ⲙ̅·ⲙⲁ·   ⲛ·ⲱⲁ[

ϣ[ⲁ]   ⲙ̣[ⲙⲁ   ⲛ̅₂ⲱⲧ̅ⲡ]′   ⲧⲁ·ⲓ·   ⲧⲉ·   ⲑⲉ′   ⲉ·ⲧⲉϥ·[

20 ⲛⲏⲩ   ⲛ̅6ⲓ   ⲡⲉⲭ̅ⲥ̅   ⲉⲣ]ⲉ   ⲛⲉϥ·ⲁⲅ·ⲅⲉ·ⲗⲟⲥ·

ⲧⲏⲣⲟⲩ   ⲕⲱⲧⲉ   ⲉⲣⲟϥ]   ϥ̣[ⲛⲁ₂ⲟ]ⲩ·   ⲧⲟ·ⲟⲧϥ·   ₂ⲱ·

---

11 ⲣⲟϥ Sa³* | 14 ⲣⲟϥ Sa³*

2 ϫⲉ ⲛⲉⲩ† Sa³: ⲁⲧⲙ̅† Ach | 6 ϫⲉ Sa³: ⲡⲣ ⲉⲩϫⲟⲩ ⲙ̅ⲙⲁⲥ Ach |
ⲧⲏⲩⲧ̅ⲛ Sa³: om Ach † ⲛ̅ⲧⲉⲧ̅ⲛ6ⲱ Sa³: ⲧⲉⲧⲛ₂ⲱⲡⲉ Ach | 7 ₂ⲣⲁⲓ̈
ⲛ̅ⲧⲉ Sa³: om Ach | 9 ⲟⲩⲟⲛ Sa³ᵛⁱᵈ: 6ⲉ ⲡϣⲏⲣⲉ ⲛ̅ⲧⲁⲛⲟⲙⲓⲁ Ach |
10 ⲁⲗⲗⲁ Sa³ᵛⁱᵈ: om Ach | 11-12 ⲉϥϣⲁⲛⲉⲓ – ⲡⲉⲭ̅ⲥ̅ Sa³: ⲡⲭ̅ⲥ̅
ⲁϥϣⲁⲉⲓ Ach | 12-13 ⲛ̅ⲛⲟⲩⲙⲉ₂ⲁⲗ Sa³: ⲛ̅ⲟⲩⲥⲁⲙⲛ̅ⲧ Ach | 13
ⲡⲉϥ·ⲕⲗⲟⲙ Sa³: ⲡⲕⲗⲁⲙ Ach | 15 ⲉⲣⲉ- Sa³: ⲉ- Ach | 16 ₂ⲁ
ⲧⲉϥ₂ⲏ Sa³: ₂ⲛⲧϥ Ach | 17 ⲉⲣⲉ- Sa³: ⲉ- Ach | ⲛⲁⲩ Sa³:
ⲛⲁⲛⲟ Ach | 18-19 ₂ⲛ̅ – ϣⲁ ⲙ̅ⲙⲁ Sa³ᵛⁱᵈ: ϫⲛ̅ ⲛ̅ⲥⲁ ⲙⲡ̅ⲣ̅ⲣⲓⲉ ϣⲁ ⲛ̅ⲥⲁ
Ach | 20 ⲛ̅6ⲓ ⲡⲉⲭ̅ⲥ̅ Sa³ᵛⁱᵈ: om Ach |

[12]

has sent us, that the land might not be devastated." He will

command that no king be given them for three

years and six months. The land will be

full of prosperity and great plenty.

5   The living will go to meet the dead

(and say), "Rise up and remain

with us in this state of bliss." In the

fourth year of that king

there will appear one who says,

10   "I am the Christ," but he is not. Do

not believe him. But when the Christ

comes, he comes in the manner of a bevy

of doves with his crown

of doves encircling him, as he walks

15   on the vaults of heaven, with the sign

of the cross preceding him,

while the whole world sees him like

the sun which shines from east

to west. This is the way in which

20   the Christ comes, with all his

angels surrounding him. The lawless one, however,

ι [г]

ⲱϥ ⲟⲛ] ⲛ̄ϥ·ⲁ·ⲍ ⲉ· ⲉ·ⲣⲁⲧϥ̄′ ⲍ̄ⲙ· ⲡⲙⲁ· ⲉ·ⲧⲟⲩ·ⲁ·ⲗⲃ
ⲛ̄ϭⲓ ⲡ]ϣⲏ·ⲣ ⲉ· ⲛ̄·ⲧⲁ·ⲛⲟ·ⲙⲓ·ⲁ′ ϥⲛⲁ·ⲭⲟ·ⲟⲥ′ ⲙ̄·ⲡⲣⲏ′
ⲭ ⲉ] ⲍ ⲉ· ⲁⲩ·ⲱ· ϥⲛⲁ·ⲍ ⲉ· ⲁ·ⲣⲓ· ⲕⲁ·ⲕⲉ′ ⲛ̄ϥ·ⲉⲓ·ⲣ ⲉ′ ⲁ·ⲣⲓ·
ⲟⲩ·
ⲟⲉ]ⲓ̣ⲛ ⲛ̄ϥ·ⲉⲓ·ⲣ ⲉ′ ϥⲛⲁ·ⲃⲱⲕ ⲙ̄ⲛ·ⲙⲁⲩ· ⲉ·ⲃⲟⲗ· ⲍ̄ⲛ·
5 ⲧ]ⲡ ⲉ′ ⲛ̄ϥ·ⲭⲟ·ⲟⲥ′ ⲭ ⲉ· ⲙⲟ·ⲟ·ϣ ⲉ· ⲍⲓ·ⲭ̄ⲛ· ⲑⲁ·ⲗⲁⲥ·ⲥⲁ′
ⲙ̣̄ⲛ′ ⲛ̄·ⲉ̣·ⲣⲱ·ⲟⲩ′ ⲛ̄·[ⲑ]ⲉ· ⲙ̄·ⲡⲉ·ⲧϣⲟⲩ·ⲱ·ⲟⲩ′ ϥⲛⲁ·
ⲧ]ⲣ ⲉ· ⲛ̄·ϭⲁ·ⲗ ⲉ·ⲩ·ⲉⲩ· ⲙⲟ·ⲟ·ϣ ⲉ· ϥⲛⲁ·ⲧⲣ ⲉ· ⲛ̄·ⲕϣ·
ⲫⲟ]ⲥ· ⲥⲱ·ⲧ̄ⲙ′ ϥⲛⲁ·ⲧⲣ ⲉ· ⲙ̄·ⲡⲟ· ϣⲁ·ⲭ ⲉ· ϥⲛⲁ·
ⲧⲣ ⲉ· ⲛ̄ⲃ·ⲃⲗ̄·ⲗ ⲉ· ⲛⲁⲩ· ⲉ·ⲃⲟⲗ′ ⲛ̄·ⲛⲉⲧ·ⲥⲟ̄ϥ̄ⲍ′ ϥⲛⲁ·
10 ⲧ̄ⲃ·ⲃⲟ·ⲟⲩ′ ⲛ̄·ⲛⲉⲧ·ϣⲱ·ⲛ ⲉ· ϥⲛⲁ·ⲧ̄ⲗ·ϭⲟ·ⲟⲩ′ ⲛ̄·ⲛ ⲉ·
ⲧⲟ]· ⲛⲁⲁⲓ·ⲙⲟ·ⲛⲓ·ⲟⲛ′ ϥⲛⲁ·ⲛⲟ·ⲭⲟⲩ· ⲉ·ⲃⲟⲗ′
ϥ]ⲛ̣ⲁ·ⲧⲁ·ϣⲟ· ⲛ̄·ⲛⲉϥ·ⲙⲁ·ⲉⲓⲛ′ ⲙ̄ⲛ· ⲛⲉϥ·ϣⲡⲏ·
ⲣ ⲉ· ⲙ̄·[ⲡ ⲉ]ⲙ·ⲧⲟ· ⲉ·ⲃⲟⲗ′ ⲛ̄·ⲟⲩ·ⲟ·ⲛ ⲛⲓⲙ′ ϥⲛⲁ·
ⲉ]ⲓ̣·ⲣ ⲉ· ⲛ̄·ⲛⲉⲍ·ⲃ̣[ⲏⲩ ⲉ]′ [ⲛ̄]ⲧⲁ·ⲡ[ⲉ]ⲭ̣ⲣ̄ⲏ·ⲥⲧⲟⲥ′[
15 ⲁ]ⲁ̣ⲩ′ ϣⲁ·ⲧⲛ̄· ⲧⲟ̣[ⲩⲛⲉⲥ ⲟⲩⲣⲉϥⲙⲟⲟⲩ]ⲧ̣′ ⲙ̄·ⲙⲁ·[
ⲧ ⲉ· ⲍ̄ⲙ· ⲡⲁ·ï· ⲉ·[ⲧ ⲉⲧ̄ⲛⲁⲥⲟⲩⲱⲛ]ϥ̣· ⲭ ⲉ· ⲛ̄·ⲧⲟϥ[
ⲡ ⲉ· ⲡϣⲏ·ⲣ ⲉ· ⲛ̄·ⲧ[ⲁⲛⲟⲙⲓⲁ ⲭ ⲉ ⲙ̄ⲛ]· ϭⲟⲙ· ⲙ̄[
ⲙⲟϥ′ ⲉ·ϯ· ⲛⲟⲩ·ⲯ[ⲩⲭⲏ ⲉⲓⲥ ⲛ ⲉϥⲙⲁ]ⲉⲓⲛ′ ⲅⲁⲣ̣[
ϯⲛ]ⲁ·ⲭⲟ·ⲟ̣ⲩ· ⲉ·ⲣⲱ[ⲧ̄ⲛ ⲭ ⲉ ⲉⲧ ⲉⲧ̄ⲛⲁⲥⲟⲩⲱⲛϥ̄
20 ⲟⲩⲡⲉⲗ]ⲏϭ′ ⲛ̄·ⲟⲩ·[ⲕⲟⲩⲓ ⲡ ⲉ ⲛ̄ⲥⲁⲗⲗⲁϣⲓ ⲉ
ⲛ̄]ϣⲁ·ⲙⲁ̣·ⲣⲁⲧ[ϥ̄ ⲉ ⲟⲩⲛ ⲟⲩⲧⲟ ⲛ̄ϭⲓⲙ ⲍⲓ ⲑⲏ

---

6 ⲡⲉⲧϣⲟⲩⲱⲟⲩ Sa³* | 7 ⲛ̄ϭⲁⲗ ⲉⲩ Sa³ * | 10 ϣⲱ Sa³* |

1 ⲛ̄ϥⲁⲍ ⲉ - ⲉⲧⲟⲩⲁⲁⲃ Sa³: tr post ⲁⲛⲟⲙⲓⲁ Ach | ⲛ̄ϥⲁⲍ ⲉ Sa³: ⲗⲱⲍ ⲉ
Ach | ⲍ̄ⲙ ⲡⲙⲁ Sa³: ⲍⲛ ⲙ̄ⲙⲁ Ach | 3 ⲁⲩⲱ ϥⲛⲁⲍ ⲉ Sa³ Sa¹: ϥⲍⲉïⲉ Ach
| 3-4 ⲁⲣⲓ (pr ϥⲛⲁⲭⲟⲟⲥ ⲭ ⲉ Ach) ⲕⲁⲕⲉ ⲛ̄ϥ ⲉⲓⲣ ⲉ / ⲁⲣⲓ (pr ϥⲛⲁⲭⲟⲟⲥ
ⲭ ⲉ Ach) ⲟⲩⲟ ⲉⲓ ⲛ ⲛ̄ϥ ⲉⲓⲣ ⲉ Sa³: tr Ach | 4 ⲛ̄ϥ ⲉⲓⲣ ⲉ Sa³: + ϥⲛⲁⲭⲟⲟⲥ
ⲙⲡⲟⲟ ⲍ ⲭ ⲉ ⲉⲣⲓ ⲥⲛⲁϥ ϥ ⲉⲓⲣ ⲉ Ach | 5 ⲛ̄ϥⲭⲟⲟⲥ (ⲉ ϥⲭⲱ ⲙ̄ⲙⲟⲥ Sa¹) ⲭ ⲉ
ⲙⲟⲟϣ ⲉ Sa³ Sa¹: ϥⲛⲁⲙⲁⲗⲁ ⲍ ⲉ Ach | ⲍ ⲓ ⲭ̄ⲛ Sa³ Ach: ⲡ̣ⲣ ⲍ ⲓ ⲭ̄ⲙ
ⲡ ⲉⲧϣⲟⲩⲱⲟⲩ ⲁⲩⲱ ⲧ ⲉⲧⲛ̄ⲙⲟⲟϣ ⲉ Sa¹ | 7 ⲕⲱⲫⲟⲥ Sa³ = Sa¹: ⲥⲱ ⲍ Ach |
8 ⲙ̄ⲡⲟ Sa³: ⲛ̄ⲉ ⲃ ⲟⲟⲩ ⲉ Sa¹: ⲛ ⲉ ⲃ ⲱ Ach | 9 ⲃⲃⲗ̄ⲗ ⲉ Sa³: ⲃⲗ̄ⲗ ⲉⲩ ⲉ
Sa¹ = Ach | 11 ϥⲛⲁⲛⲟⲭⲟⲩ Sa³ Sa¹: ϥⲛⲁⲧ ⲉ ⲕⲟⲩ Ach | 12-13 ϣⲡⲏⲣ ⲉ
Sa³ Sa¹: ⲙⲁï ⲍ ⲉ Ach | 14-15 ⲛ̄ⲧⲁ ... ⲁⲁⲩ Sa³ᵛⁱᵈ = Ach: ⲉⲧ ⲉⲣ ⲉ
ⲡⲭⲥ̅ ⲛ̄ⲛⲁ ⲉ ⲟⲟⲩ ⲉ Sa¹ | 15 ϣⲁⲧ̄ⲛ Sa³ Sa¹: ⲥⲁ ⲃ ⲗ̄ⲗ ⲉ Ach | 15-16 ⲙ̄ⲙⲁⲧ ⲉ
Sa³ Sa¹: ⲟⲩⲗⲉ ⲉ ⲧϥ Ach | 16 ⲉⲧ ⲉⲧ̄ⲛⲁⲥⲟⲩⲱⲛϥ Sa³ = Ach: ⲧ ⲉⲧ ⲛ ⲁⲥⲟⲩⲱⲛϥ
Sa¹ | 18 ⲛ̣ⲟ̣ⲩⲯⲩⲭⲏ Sa³: ⲯⲩⲭⲏ Sa¹ Ach | ⲅⲁⲣ Sa³ Ach: om Sa¹ |
19 ⲭ ⲉ Sa³ᵛⁱᵈ = Ach: ⲭ ⲉⲕⲁⲁⲥ Sa¹ | 20 ⲡⲉⲗ ⲏϭ Sa³ᵛⁱᵈ Ach: ⲡ ⲉⲗ ⲏ ⲕ
Sa¹ | ⲛ̄ⲟⲩⲕⲟⲩⲓ Sa³ⁱⁿᶜ = Sa¹: ⲛ̄ⲟⲩⲍ ⲏ ⲙ Ach |

[13]

will proceed to take his stand

in the holy place. He will say to the sun,

"Fall," and it falls, "Be dark," and it complies, "Shine,"

and it does. He will accompany them through

5 the sky and say, "Walk upon the sea

and upon the rivers as though they were dry land." He will

make the lame walk. He will make the deaf

hear. He will make the dumb speak. He will

make the blind see. Lepers he will

10 heal. The sick he will cure. The

demon-possessed he will exorcize.

He will multiply his signs and wonders

in everyone's presence. He will do

the things which the Christ did,

15 with the sole exception of raising the dead.

By this you will know that he

is the lawless one: he has no

power to give souls. Now his signs

I will tell you in order that you may recognize him.

20 He is a little peleč, tall (?)

thinlegged, with a tuft of grey hair on his forehead

↑ ‾

ΙΑ

Ⲛ· [ⲭⲱϥ]

Ⲛ·ϭⲁⲗ·ⲟⲩ·ⲃⲧ̄ⲃ̄′ ⲉ·ⲣⲉ· Ⲛ·ⲛⲉϥ·ⲃⲟⲩ·ⲍⲉ· ⲛⲏ·[ⲩ ϣⲁ

ⲛⲉϥ·ⲙ̄ⲛ̄ⲙⲁ·ⲁ·ⲭⲉ̣′ ⲉ·ⲟⲩ·ⲛ ⲟⲩ·ⲧⲟ· Ⲛ·ⲥⲱⲃ̄ⲃ̄· ⲍⲓ[ⲟⲏ

Ⲛ·ⲛⲉϥ·ϭⲓⲝ′ ϥⲛⲁ·ϣⲃ·ⲧ̄ϥ̄′ Ⲙ̄·ⲡⲉ·ⲧ̄ⲛ̄·Ⲙ̄·ⲡⲧⲟ[

ⲉ·ⲃⲟⲗ′ ⲍ̄ⲛ̄·ⲥⲟⲡ· ⲙⲉⲛ′ ϥⲛⲁ·ⲣ̄· ⲍ̄ⲗ·ⲗⲟ′ ⲍⲉⲛ·ⲥⲟⲡ[

5 ⲁⲉ ⲟⲛ· ϥⲛⲁ·ⲣ̄· ϣⲏ·ⲣⲉ· ϣⲏⲙ′ ϥⲛⲁ·ϣⲃ̄ⲧϥ′ ⲍ̄Ⲙ̄[

ⲙⲁ·ⲉ[ⲓ]ⲛ· ⲛⲓⲙ′ ⲙⲁ·ⲉⲓⲛ· ⲁⲉ· Ⲛ̄·ⲧⲟϥ′ Ⲛ̄·ⲧⲉϥ·[

ⲁ·[ⲡ]ⲉ′ Ⲛ̄·ⲛⲉϥ·ϣⲱ̄ⲃ·ⲧⲟⲩ′ ⲍ̄Ⲙ̄· ⲡⲁ·ï· ⲉ·ⲧⲉ·ⲧⲛⲁ[

ⲥⲟⲩ·ϣⲛϥ′ ⲭⲉ· Ⲛ̄·ⲧⲟϥ· ⲡⲉ· ⲡϣⲏ·ⲣⲉ· Ⲛ̄ⲧⲁⲛⲟ̣

ⲙⲓ·ⲁ′ ⲥⲛ̄·ⲛⲁ·ⲥⲱ·ⲧ̄Ⲙ̄· Ⲛ̄·ϭⲓ· ⲧⲡⲁⲣ·ⲑⲉ·ⲛ[ⲟⲥ

10 ⲉ·ⲧⲉ· ⲡⲉⲥ·ⲣⲁⲛ· ⲡⲉ′ ⲧⲁ·ⲃⲓ·ⲑⲁ ⲭⲉ· ⲁ·ⲡⲁⲧϣⲓⲛ[ⲉ

ⲟⲩⲟⲛⲍ̄ϥ̄· ⲉ·ⲃⲟⲗ′ ⲍ̄Ⲛ̄· Ⲙ̄·ⲙⲁ· ⲉ·ⲧⲟⲩ·ⲁ·ⲁⲃ′ ⲥⲛ̣[ⲁ

ϭⲟ·ⲗⲉⲥ′ Ⲙ̄·ⲡⲉⲥ·ⲍⲃⲟⲥ′ Ⲛ̄·ϣⲏⲥ̄′ ⲛ̣ⲥ̣·ⲡⲱ[ⲧ

ⲉ]ⲍⲣⲁ·ï′ ⲉ·†[.].ⲟⲩⲁ̣[ⲗⲓⲁ ⲛ̄ⲧ̄ⲥ·ⲥⲟ·ⲟ·ⲍⲉ′ Ⲙ̄[ⲙⲟϥ

ϣⲁⲍⲣⲁ·ï̈ [ⲉⲑⲓⲉⲣⲟⲩⲥⲁⲗⲏ]Ⲙ′ ⲉⲥ·ⲭⲱ· Ⲙ̄[ⲙⲟⲥ

15 ⲛⲁϥ· ⲭⲉ· ⲱ [ⲡⲁⲧϣⲓⲛⲉ ⲱ] ⲡϣⲏ·ⲣⲉ· Ⲛ̄·ⲧⲁ[

ⲛⲟ·ⲙⲓ·ⲁ′ ⲱ [ⲡⲉⲧⲁϥⲣ̄ ⲭ]ⲁ̣·ⲭⲉ ⲉ·ⲛⲉ·ⲧⲟⲩ·ⲁ·[

ⲁ]ⲃ ⲧⲏ·ⲣⲟⲩ [ⲧⲟⲧⲉ ϥⲛⲁϭⲱ]ⲛ̄ⲧ′ ⲉⲧ·ⲡⲁⲣⲑⲉ[

ⲛⲟⲥ Ⲛ̄ϭⲓ ⲡⲁⲧϣⲓⲛⲉ ϥ]ⲛⲁ·ⲡⲱⲧ· Ⲛ̄·ⲥ̣[ⲱⲥ

ϣⲁⲍⲣⲁ·ï̈ ⲉⲙⲙⲁ Ⲛ̄ⲍⲱⲧⲡ] Ⲙ̄·ⲡⲣⲡ̣[ⲏ ϥⲛⲁ

20 ⲥⲱⲛⲧ̄ Ⲙ̄ⲡⲉⲥⲥⲛⲟϥ] Ⲙ̄·ⲡⲛⲁⲩ [Ⲛ̄

ⲣⲟⲩⲍⲉ Ⲛ̄ϥⲛⲟⲩⲭⲉ Ⲙ̄]ⲙⲟⲥ′ ⲉ·ⲍⲣⲁ[ï̈

9 ⲥⲛ̄ⲁ(ⲁⲥⲱⲧⲙ̄) Sa³*: ⲥⲛ̄ⲛ(ⲁⲥⲱⲧⲙ̄) Sa³ᶜ | 10 ⲡⲉⲣⲁⲛ Sa³*

1 Ⲛ̄ϭⲁⲗⲟⲩⲃ̄ⲧ̄ⲃ̄ Sa³ Sa¹: Ⲛ̄ϣⲁⲧⲙⲉⲍⲏⲗ Ach | ⲉⲣⲉ Sa³ Sa¹: om Ach |
ⲛⲉϥⲃⲟⲩⲍⲉ Sa³: ⲛⲉϥⲛ̄₂ Sa¹ Ach | 2 ⲟⲩⲧⲟ Sa³: ⲟⲩⲕⲱⲕ Sa¹ = Ach 3
Ⲙ̄ⲡⲉⲧ̄ⲛ̄ Sa³ = Sa¹: om Ach | 4-5 ⲍ̄Ⲛ̄(ⲍⲓⲛ Sa¹)-ⲟⲛ Sa³ Sa¹
(ⲍⲉⲛⲥⲟⲡ: ⲍⲓⲛⲕⲉ<ⲥ>ⲟⲡ Sa¹): Ⲛ̄ⲛⲉⲧⲥⲁⲛⲧ Ⲛ̄ⲥⲱϥ Ach | 5 ϣⲏⲣⲉ Sa³
Ach: om Sa¹ | ϣⲏⲙ Sa³ Sa¹: + ϥⲛⲁⲣ̄ ⲍ̄ⲗⲗⲟ Ach | 5-6 ⲍ̄Ⲙ ⲙⲁⲉⲓⲛ
ⲛⲓⲙ Sa³ = Ach: ⲍ̄Ⲛ̄ ⲛⲉϥⲙⲁⲉⲓⲛ Sa¹ | 6 ⲁⲉ Sa³ Sa¹: om Ach | 7
Ⲛ̄ⲛⲉϥϣⲱ̄ⲃⲧⲟⲩ Sa³: ϥⲛⲁϣⲃ̄ⲧⲟⲩ ⲁⲛ Sa¹: ⲛⲟⲩⲍϣⲓⲃⲉ Ach | 11
ⲟⲩⲟⲛⲍ̄ϥ̄ Sa³ = Ach: ⲟⲩⲱⲛⲍ̄₂ Sa¹ | Ⲙ̄ⲙⲁ Sa³ Ach: ⲡⲙⲁ Sa¹ | 11-12
ⲥⲛⲁϭⲟⲗⲉⲥ Sa³ = Sa¹: ⲥⲉⲃⲁⲗⲗⲉⲥ Ach | 13 ⲉⲍⲣⲁï̈ Sa³ᵛⁱᵈ Sa¹:
Ⲛ̄ⲥⲱϥ ϣⲁⲍⲣⲏï̈ Ach | 14 ϣⲁⲍⲣⲁï̈ ⲉⲑⲓⲉⲣⲟⲩⲥⲁⲗⲏⲙ Sa³ᵛⁱᵈ: (ϥ)ϣⲁ
ⲁⲍⲣⲁï̈ ⲉⲝⲓⲉⲑⲓⲉⲗⲏⲙ Sa¹: ϣⲁ ⲧⲍⲓⲉⲣⲟⲩⲥⲁⲗⲏⲙ Ach: ⲉⲥⲭⲱ Ⲙ̄ⲙⲟⲥ
Sa³ Sa¹: om Ach | 15 ⲛⲁϥ Sa³: om Sa¹ Ach |

[14]

like one who is bald. His eyelids extend to

his ears. He has leprosy on

his hands. He will change himself before you.

At one time he will be an old man; at another,

5 he will be a young child. He will change himself with

every sign, but the aspect of his head

he will not be able to change. By this you will

know that he is the lawless one.

The young woman whose name is Tabitha

10 will hear that the shameless one

has made his appearance in the holy places. She will

dress in her linen clothes and hurry

to Judaea and reprove him

as far as Jerusalem, and say

15 to him, "O you shameless one, O you lawless

one, O you enemy of all

the saints!" Then the shameless one will become

angry with the young woman. He will pursue her

to the region of the setting of the sun. He will

20 suck her blood in the

evening and toss her onto

$\overline{\text{i}[6]}$

→

ⲉⲝⲛ] ⲡ⳰ⲣ·ⲡⲉ′ ⲛⲥ·ϣⲱⲡⲉ′ ⲛ̄·ⲟⲩ·ϫⲁ·ⲓ̈· ⲙ̄·ⲡ[ⲗⲁⲟ]ⲥ′

ⲥⲛⲁⲧ]ⲱ·ⲟⲩⲛⲥ· ⲛ̄·ⲡ·ⲛ̣ⲁ̣ⲩ′ ⲛ̄·ϣⲱ·ⲣⲡ′ ⲉ·ⲥⲟ·ⲛ̣[ⲍ ⲛ̄ⲧ̄ⲥ·

ⲥⲟ]ⲟ·[ⲍⲉ]· ⲛ̄·ⲙⲟϥ′ ⲉⲥ·ϫⲱ· ⲙ̄·ⲙⲟⲥ· ϫⲉ· ⲡⲁⲧϣ[ⲓ]ⲡ̣ⲉ′

ⲙ̄ⲧ̄ⲛ· ϭ[ⲟ]ⲙ· ⲛ̄·ⲙⲟⲕ· ⲉⲧⲁ·ⲯⲩ·ⲭⲏ′ ⲟⲩ·ⲗⲉ· ⲡⲁ·ⲥⲱ·ⲙⲁ′

5   ϫ]ⲉ· ϯⲟⲛ⳰ⲍ· ⲁ·ⲛⲟⲕ̣· ϩⲙ̄· ⲡϫⲟ·ⲉⲓⲥ̣′ ⲛ̄·ⲟⲩ·ⲟ·ⲉⲓϣ· ⲛⲓⲙ′

ⲡⲁ·ⲕⲉ·ⲥⲛⲟϥ′ ⲛ̄·ⲁ[ⲉ] ⲟⲛ′ ⲉⲛ·ⲧⲁⲕ·ⲛ[ⲟ]ⲩϫⲉ ⲙ̄·ⲙⲟϥ′

ⲉⲝⲧ̄ⲙ̣· ⲡ⳰ⲣ·ⲡⲉ′ ⲁϥ·ϣⲱ·ⲡⲉ· ⲛ̄·[ⲟ]ⲩ·ϫⲁ·ⲓ̈· ⲙ̄·ⲡⲗⲁ·ⲟⲥ′

ⲧ]ⲟⲧ̣ⲉ̣· ⲉϥϣⲁⲛⲥⲱ·ⲧⲙ̄· ⲛ̄·ϭⲓ· ϩⲏ·ⲗⲓ·ⲁⲥ· ⲙⲛ̄· ⲉ·

ⲛ̣ⲱⲭ· ϫⲉ· ⲁ·ⲡⲁ·ⲧϣⲓ·ⲡⲉ′ ⲟⲩ·ⲟⲛ⳰ⲍ· ⲉ·ⲃⲟⲗ′ ϩⲛ̄·

10 ⲙ̄ⲙⲁ· ⲉ·ⲧⲟⲩ·ⲁ·ⲁⲃ′ ⲥⲉ·ⲛ̣[ⲏ]ⲩ· ⲉ·ⲡⲉ·ⲥⲏⲧ′ ⲛ̄·ⲥⲉ·

ⲡⲟ·ⲗⲉ·ⲙⲉⲓ· ⲙⲛ̄·ⲙⲁϥ′ ⲉⲩ·ϫ[ⲱ]· ⲙ̄·ⲙⲟⲥ· ⲛⲁϥ· ϫⲉ·

ⲛ̄ⲕⲱ]ⲓ̣ⲡⲉ· ⲁⲛ· ⲭ̣[ⲉ] ⲕⲟ. ⲛ̄·ϣⲙ̄·ⲙⲟ· ⲛ̄·ⲟⲩ·

ⲟⲉⲓϣ] ⲛⲓⲙ ⲁ·ⲕ⳿ⲧⲣ̄ ϫ]ⲁ̣ϫⲉ· ⲉ·ⲛⲁⲧ[ⲡⲉ ⲁ]ⲩⲱ′

ⲁ·ⲕⲉⲓⲣ]ⲉ· ⲉ·ⲛ[ⲉⲧ]ϩⲓ·ⲝ̄ⲙ· ⲡⲕⲁϩ′ ⲁ·[ⲕⲣ̄ ϫ]ⲁ·

15 ϫⲉ· ⲉ]ⲛ̄ⲁⲅ[ⲅⲉⲗⲟ]ⲥ̣′ ⲙⲛ̄· ⲛⲉ·ⲑⲣ[ⲟⲛⲟⲥ] ⲛ̄ⲧ̄ⲕ ⲟ[ⲩ

ϣⲙ̣[ⲙ]ⲟ· ⲛ̄·ⲛ[ⲟⲩⲟⲉⲓϣ] ⲛ̣ⲓ̣ⲙ′ ⲁ[ⲕϩⲉ ⲉⲃⲟ]ⲗ ϩⲛ̄[

ⲧ]ⲡⲉ ⲛ̄·ⲑⲉ· ⲙ̄[ⲛ̄ⲥⲓⲟⲩ ⲛ̄ⲍⲧⲟ]ⲟⲩ·ⲉ· ⲁ[ⲕⲱⲓⲃ]ⲉ′ ⲁ

]ⲧⲉⲕ·ⲫⲩ[ⲗⲏ ⲣ̄ ⲕⲁ]·ⲕⲉ· ⲉ·[ⲣⲟⲕ ⲛ̄ⲧ̄ϣ[ⲓⲡⲉ

ⲣⲱ· ⲁⲛ′ ⲛ̄·ⲧ[ⲟⲕ ⲉⲕⲧⲱⲕ ⲙ̄ⲙⲟⲕ ⲉⲡⲛⲟⲩ

20 ⲧⲉ] ⲛ̄·ⲧⲟ·ⲟⲕ· ⲡ[ⲇⲓⲁⲃⲟⲗⲟⲥ ϥⲛⲁⲥⲱⲧ̄ⲙ

ⲛ̄ϭⲓ]ⲓ̣· ⲡⲁⲧ[ϣⲓⲡⲉ ⲛ̄ϥϭⲱⲛⲧ̄ ⲛ̄ϥⲡⲟⲗⲉ

---

2 ⲡⲛⲁⲩ Sa[3*] | 5 ⲛ̄ⲟⲉⲓϣ Sa[3*] | 16 ⲉⲃⲟⲥ Sa[3*] |

2 ⲥⲛⲁⲧⲱⲟⲩⲛⲥ Sa[3]: ⲥ̄ⲛⲁⲧⲱⲟⲩⲛ Sa[1] | ⲉⲥⲟⲛⲍ Sa[3]: ⲛ̄ⲥⲱⲛⲍ Sa[1] | 6 ⲛ̄ⲁⲉ ⲟⲛ Sa[3]: om Sa[1] | ⲉⲛⲧⲁⲕⲛⲟⲩϫⲉ Sa[3]: ⲁⲕⲛⲟⲩϫⲉ Sa[1] | 10 ⲙ̄ⲙⲁ Sa[3vid]: ⲡⲙⲁ Sa[1] | 11 ⲛⲁϥ Sa[3]: om Sa[1] | 12 ⲁⲛ Sa[3]: pr ⲣⲱ Sa[1] | ⲁⲛ Sa[3]: + ⲛ̄ⲧⲟⲕ ⲉⲕⲧⲱϭⲉ ⲙ̄ⲙⲟⲕ ⲛ̄ⲛⲉⲧⲟⲩⲁⲁⲃ Sa[1] | 13 ⲁⲩⲱ Sa[3vid]: om Sa[1] | 14 ⲉⲛⲉⲧϩⲓⲝ̄ⲙ Sa[3]: ⲁⲛⲁⲗ– Sa[1] | 15 ⲉⲛⲁⲅⲅⲉⲗⲟⲥ ⲙⲛ̄ ⲛⲉⲑⲣⲟⲛⲟⲥ Sa[3]: ⲁⲛⲑⲣⲟⲛⲟⲥ ⲁⲕⲉⲓⲣⲉ ⲁⲛⲁⲅⲅⲉⲗⲟⲥ Sa[1] | 18 ⲧⲉⲕⲫⲩⲗⲏ Sa[3vid]: ⲧⲉⲫⲩⲗⲏ Sa[1] | 20 ⲡⲁⲓⲁⲃⲟⲗⲟⲥ Sa[3vid]: ⲟⲩⲁⲓⲁⲃⲟⲗⲟⲥ Sa[1] |

[15]

the temple, and she will become salvation for the people.

At dawn she will rise up alive and

rebuke him saying, "You shameless one,

You have no power over my soul, nor over my body,

5   because I live in the Lord always,

and even my blood which you spilled

on the temple became salvation for the people."

Then, when Elijah and Enoch hear

that the shameless one has appeared

10   in the holy places, they will come down and

wage war against him saying,

"Are you not ashamed seeing that you are estranged

constantly? You became an enemy of heavenly beings,

now you have acted against those on earth as well. You became an

enemy

15   of angels and powers. You are

an enemy for all time. You fell from

heaven like the morning stars. You have changed.

Your substance (?) has been darkened. Are you not

now ashamed, you who hurl yourself against

20   God? You are the devil." The shameless one

will hear, become angry and wage war

↑   ⲓ︦ⲋ

ⲙ ⲓ [ⲙ︦ⲛ]ⲙ·ⲁⲩ′ ⲍ ⲓ· ⲧⲁ·ⲅⲟ︦ⲣⲁ ⲛ︦·ⲧⲛⲟ︦ⲋ ⲙ[ⲡⲟⲗ ⲓ ⲥ
ⲛ︦ϥ[ϯ ⲥ]ⲁ·ϣ︦ϥ· ⲛ︦·ⲍⲟ·ⲟⲩ′ ⲉϥ·ⲡⲟ·ⲗⲉ·ⲙ ⲉ ⲓ· ⲛ︦ⲧ︦ⲛ
ⲙ[ⲙⲁ]ⲩ′ ⲁⲩ·ⲱ ⲛ︦ϥ·ⲍⲱ·ⲧ︦ⲃ· ⲛ︦·ⲙⲟ·ⲟⲩ′ ⲛ︦ⲥ̣ⲉ[
ϯ ϣⲟⲙ′ ⲛ︦·ⲍⲟ·ⲟⲩ′ ⲟⲩ·ⲋⲟⲥ′ ⲉⲩ·ⲙⲟ·ⲟⲩⲧ ⲍ ⲓ [

5 ⲧⲁ·ⲅⲟ·ⲣⲁ′ ⲉ·ⲣⲉ· ⲡⲗⲁ·ⲟⲥ· [ⲧ]ⲏ̣ⲣ̣ϥ′ ⲛⲁⲩ ⲉⲣⲟ·ⲟⲩ[
ⲍ︦ⲙ· ⲙⲉⲍ ϥ[ⲧ]ⲟ̣·ⲟⲩ′ ⲛ︦·ⲗⲉ· ⲛ︦·ⲍⲟ[ⲟ]ⲩ′ ⲥⲉ·ⲛⲁ·ⲧ̣ⲱ̣·ⲟ̣ⲩ[
ⲛⲟⲩ· ⲟⲛ′ ⲛ︦·ⲥⲉ·ⲥⲟ·[ⲟ]·ⲍ ⲉ· ⲙ︦·ⲙⲟϥ′ ⲉⲩ·ϫⲱ′ [ⲙ︦ⲙⲟⲥ
ⲛⲁϥ ϫⲉ· ⲱ· ⲡⲁ·ⲧϣ ⲓ·ⲡⲉ· ⲛ︦ⲧ·ϣ ⲓ·ⲡⲉ· ⲣⲱ ⲁⲛ̣[
ⲛ︦·ⲧⲟⲕ′ ⲉⲕ·ⲡⲗⲁ·ⲛⲁ· ⲙ︦·ⲡⲗⲁ·ⲟⲥ· ⲙ︦ⲡⲛⲟⲩⲧ̣[ⲉ

10 ⲡⲁ·ⲓ̈· ⲉ·ⲧⲉ·ⲙ︦ⲛⲉⲕ[ϣ]ⲉⲛ· ⲍ ⲓ·ⲥⲉ· ⲉⲣⲟϥ′ ⲛ︦ⲧ·ⲥⲟ̣[
ⲟⲩⲛ· ⲣ̣ⲱ· ⲁⲛ′ ⲛ︦·ⲧ̣[ⲟ]ⲕ̣′ ϫⲉ· ⲧⲛ·ⲟⲛ︦ⲍ· ⲍ︦ⲙ· ⲡ·ⲭ̣[ⲟ
ⲉ ⲓ ⲥ′ ⲉⲛ·ⲉ̣ⲥⲟ·ⲟ·ⲍ ⲉ [ⲙ︦]ⲙⲟⲕ̣ ⲛⲟⲩⲟ·ⲉ̣[ⲓ ϣ]· [ⲛ ⲓ ⲙ
ⲉⲕ·ϫ̣[ⲱ ⲙ︦]·ⲙⲟⲥ′ ϫⲉ· ⲁ[ⲓ ⲋ]ⲙ︦·ⲋⲟⲙ [ⲉ︦ⲍ︦ⲣⲁ̈ ⲓ
ⲉ·ϫ︦ⲛ [ⲛⲁ̈ ⲓ] ϯ︦ⲛ·ⲛⲁ·ⲕⲱ′ ⲉ·ⲍ[ⲣⲁ̈ ⲓ] ⲛ︦·ⲧⲥⲁⲣ[ⲝ ⲛ︦

15 ⲡⲉ·ⲓ̈[ⲥⲱⲙ]ⲁ′ ⲛ︦·ⲧ︦ⲛ·ⲍ̣ⲱ[ⲧ︦ⲃ ⲙ︦]·ⲙⲟⲕ̣ [ⲉ︦ⲙ︦ⲛ
ⲋⲟⲙ̣ [ⲙ︦ⲙⲟ]ⲕ̣′ ⲉ̣·ϣⲁ̣ⲝ[ⲉ ⲍ]ⲙ̣· ⲡⲉ·ⲍ[ⲟ]ⲟ̣ⲩ[
ⲉ]·ⲧ︦ⲙ[ⲙⲁ]ⲩ′ ϫⲉ· ⲧ︦ⲛ̣[ⲱⲛ︦ⲍ ⲍ︦ⲙ] ⲡⲭⲟ·ⲉ ⲓ ⲥ[
ⲛ︦]·[ⲟⲩⲟⲉ ⲓ]·ϣ′ ⲛ ⲓ ⲙ [ϫⲉ ⲕⲟ] ⲛ︦·ⲭⲁ·ⲭ̣ⲉ· ⲛ︦[
ⲟⲩⲟⲉ ⲓ ϣ ⲛ ⲓ ⲙ ϥⲛⲁⲥⲱ]ⲧ︦ⲙ ⲛ︦·ⲋ ⲓ· ⲡⲁ̣[ⲧ

20 ϣ ⲓ ⲛⲉ ⲉϥⲋⲱⲛ︦ⲧ ⲛ︦ϥⲡⲟⲗ]ⲉ̣·ⲙⲉ ⲓ· ⲛ︦ⲙ·ⲙ[ⲁⲩ
ⲧⲡⲟⲗ ⲓ ⲥ ⲧⲏⲣ︦ⲥ ⲛ︦ⲁⲕⲱⲧⲉ ⲉ]· ⲣⲟ·ⲟⲩ′ ⲍ︦ⲧ̣ⲙ̣

_____

6 ⲍⲟⲟⲩ Sa³* | 12 ⲉⲛⲥⲟⲟⲍⲉ Sa³* |

3 ⲁⲩⲱ – ⲙ︦ⲙⲟⲟⲩ Sa³: om Sa¹ | 6 ⲍ︦ⲙ ⲙⲉⲍϥⲧⲟⲟⲩ Sa³: ⲍ︦ⲛ
ⲡⲙⲁⲍϥⲧⲟⲟⲩ Sa¹ | ⲛ︦ⲗⲉ Sa³: ⲗⲉ Sa¹ | 6-7 ⲥⲉⲛⲁⲧⲱⲟⲩⲛⲟⲩ Sa³:
ⲥⲉⲛⲁⲧⲱⲟⲩⲛ Sa¹ | 7 ⲟⲛ Sa³: om Sa¹ | 8 ⲛⲁϥ Sa³: om Sa¹ |
ⲡⲁⲧϣ ⲓ ⲛⲉ Sa³ Sa¹: + ⲱ ⲡϣⲏⲣ ⲉ ⲛ︦ⲧⲁⲛⲟⲙ ⲓ ⲁ Ach | 9 ⲛ︦ⲧⲟⲕ Sa³inc
Ach: pr ϫⲉ Sa¹ | ⲙ︦ⲡⲛⲟⲩⲧⲉ Sa³ Ach: ⲙ︦ⲡⲛ︦ⲛⲟⲩⲧⲉ Sa¹ | 11 ⲣⲱ
ⲁⲛ Sa³: tr Sa¹: om ⲣⲱ Ach | 12 ⲉⲛⲉⲥⲟⲟⲍⲉ Sa³: ⲉⲥⲱⲟⲍⲉ Sa¹
| 12-13 ⲉⲛⲉⲥⲟⲟⲍⲉ – ⲉ︦ⲍ︦ⲣⲁ̈ ⲓ Sa³ Sa¹ (ⲉⲥⲱⲟⲍⲉ–): ⲉⲩⲭⲟⲩ ⲛ︦ϣⲉⲭⲉ
ⲁⲩⲋⲛ︦ⲋⲁⲙ ⲁⲣⲁϥ ⲉⲩⲭⲟⲩ ⲙ︦ⲙⲁⲥ ϫⲉ Ach | 15 ⲡⲉ ⲓ̈ⲥⲱⲙⲁ Sa³ᵛⁱᵈ = Sa¹:
ⲡ︦ⲡ︦ⲛ︦ⲁ Ach | 17 ⲧ︦ⲛⲱ︦ⲛ︦ⲍ Sa³inc Sa¹: ⲧ︦ⲛⲭⲱⲣ ⲉ Ach | 17-18 ⲍ︦ⲙ
ⲡⲭⲟⲉ ⲓ ⲥ / ⲛ︦ⲟⲩⲟⲉ ⲓ ϣ ⲛ ⲓ ⲙ Sa³ = Sa¹: tr Ach | 18 ϫⲉ Sa³ᵛⁱᵈ Sa¹:
ⲛ︦ⲧⲁⲕ ⲗⲉ Ach | ⲛ︦ⲭⲁⲭⲉ Sa³ Sa¹: + ⲁⲡⲛⲟⲩⲧⲉ Ach | 20 ⲉϥⲋⲱⲛ︦ⲧ
Sa² Sa¹: ϥ ⲃⲱⲗⲕ Ach | 21 ⲛ︦ⲁⲕⲱⲧⲉ Sa³inc Sa¹: ⲧⲉ ... ⲕⲱⲧⲉ
Ach |

[16]

against them in the market place of the great city.

He will spend seven days fighting with

them and kill them. For

three and a half days they will lie dead in

5   the market place in full view of all the people.

But on the fourth day they will arise

again and rebuke him, saying

to him, "O you shameless one, are you not ashamed,

you who deceive God's people,

10   for whom you have not suffered? Do you

not know that we live in the Lord,

in order that we may rebuke you

whenever you say, 'I have overpowered

them?' We will lay aside the flesh of

15   this body and kill you without your being

able to utter a sound at that

time, because we live in the Lord

always, whereas you are a perpetual

enemy." The shameless one will listen

20   in anger and wage war against them.

The whole city will surround them. At

ⲡⲉ₂ⲟⲟⲩ] ⲉⲧⲙⲙ[ⲁⲩ]ʼ ϭⲉˑⲛⲁˑⲱϣ [ⲗⲟⲩⲗⲁ]ˑⲓ̈ˑ ⲉ[₂ⲣⲁ̈ⲓ

ⲉⲧⲡ]ⲉ̣ʼ ⲉⲩˑⲣ̅ˑ ⲟⲩˑⲟˑⲉⲓⲛ ⲉ̣ⲣⲉˑ ⲡⲕⲟⲥˑⲙ[ⲟⲥ] ⲧⲏⲣϥ ⲛⲁⲩ

ⲉ]ⲣⲟ̣ⲟ̣[ⲩ]ʼ ⲛ̅ϥˑⲧ̅ⲙ̅ˑϣ̣ˑϭ̅ⲙ̅ϭⲟⲙˑ ⲉˑⲣⲟˑⲟ[ⲩ] ⲛ̅ϭⲓ ⲡϣⲏˑ

ⲣⲉ] ⲛ̅ˑⲧⲁˑⲛ̣ⲟˑⲙⲓˑⲁ̣ʼ ϥⲛⲁˑϭⲱⲛⲧ ⲉˑⲡ[ⲕ]ⲁ₂ʼ ⲁⲩˑⲱˑ

5 ϥ]ⲛ̣ⲁˑⲕⲱ̣ˑⲧⲉʼ ⲛ̅ˑⲥⲁ ⲣ̅ⲛⲟˑⲃⲉʼ ⲉˑⲡⲗⲗ̣ⲟˑⲟ̣[ⲥ]ʼ ϥⲛⲁˑⲕⲉˑⲗⲉ̣[ⲩ

ⲉ] ⲛ̅ˑⲥⲉˑⲣ̣ⲱⲕ₂ʼ ⲛ̅ˑⲛⲉⲩˑⲃⲁⲗʼ ₂ⲛ̅ˑ ⲟⲩϭ̣ⲁ₂ ⲛ̅ˑⲡⲉ[

ⲛⲓ]ⲡⲉʼ ϥⲛⲁˑⲉⲓˑⲛⲉ̣ˑ ⲛ̅ˑⲛ̣ⲉⲩˑⲉⲓˑⲏⲃˑ ⲟ[ⲩ]ⲁ̣ˑ ⲟⲩˑⲁʼ ϥⲛ̣[ⲁ

ⲕ̣ⲉ̣ⲗ̣[ⲉⲩⲉ]ˑ ⲛ̅ˑⲥⲉˑⲛⲉ̣ϫˑ [₂ⲙ̅]ⲭˑ ₂ⲓˑ ⲕⲟˑⲛⲓⲁʼ ⲉˑ₂ⲣⲁˑⲓ̈ˑ

ⲉˑϣⲁⲛⲧ̣[ⲟ]ⲩʼ ⲛⲏ ⲇⲉ ⲛ[ⲧⲟ]ˑⲟⲩʼ ⲉˑⲧⲉˑⲙ̅ⲡⲟⲩˑϣⲧⲱ

10 ⲟⲩⲛ̣ˑ ₂ⲁ [ⲛ̅]ⲃⲁˑⲥⲁˑⲛⲟⲥ ⲙ̅ⲡ̅ⲣ̅ˑⲣⲟˑ ⲉˑⲧ̅ⲙ̅ˑⲙⲁⲩʼ ⲥⲉˑ

ⲛⲁ]ϥ̣ⲓ ⲛ̅ⲛⲉⲩˑⲛⲟⲩⲃ [ⲛ̅ⲥⲉ]ⲡⲱⲧʼ ₂ⲓⲭⲛ̅ ⲛ̅ⲭⲓˑⲟⲣʼ

ⲉⲩⲭ]ⲱ̣ˑ ⲙ̅ˑⲙⲟⲥʼ ϫⲉˑ ϫ[ⲓⲟⲣ] ⲙ̅ˑⲙⲟⲛʼ ⲉˑⲧⲉˑⲣⲏˑⲙⲟⲥʼ

                    ⲑⲉ[ⲉ . .]ⲛ̅ⲑⲉ

ⲥⲉⲛⲁⲛ̅]ⲕ̣ⲟˑⲧⲕ̣ˑ ⲛ̅ⲟ̣[ⲩⲁ ⲛ̅]ⲟⲩⲁˑ ⲉ[ϥ₂ⲓⲛⲏⲃ

ⲉⲣ]ⲉ [ⲡ]ⲭ̣ⲟˑⲉⲓⲥˑ ⲛⲁˑϣⲉⲡ [ⲛ]ⲉ̣ⲩˑⲡ̅ⲛ̅ⲁ̅ ⲉⲣⲟϥ ⲙ̅ⲛ̅

15 ⲛⲉⲩˑⲯ[ⲩ]ⲭⲏʼ ⟦ⲙ̅ⲛ̅⟧ ⲛⲉⲩⲥⲁⲣⲝˑ ⲛⲁ[ϣⲱⲡⲉ ⲛ̅ⲟⲉ

ⲛ̅ⲛ̣ⲓˑ̣ⲡⲉⲣⲛⲁʼ ⲙ̅ⲛ̅ˑ ⲑⲏˑⲣⲓˑⲟⲛʼ ⲛⲁˑⲟ[ⲩⲟⲏⲟⲩ ϣⲁ

ⲫⲁˑⲉ̣ˑ ⲛ̅ˑ₂ⲟˑⲟⲩʼ ⲛ̅ⲧ̅ˑⲛⲟϭʼ ⲛ̅ˑⲕ̣ⲣ̣[ⲓⲥⲓⲥ ⲥⲉⲛⲁⲧⲱ

ⲟⲩⲛⲟⲩˑ ⲛ̅ˑⲥⲉˑϫⲓˑ ⲛ̅ˑ[ⲟ]ⲩˑⲙⲁˑ ⲛ̅[ⲙ̅ⲧⲟⲛ ⲁⲗⲗⲁ

ⲥⲉˑⲛⲁˑϣⲱˑⲡⲉˑ ⲁ̣ⲛ̣ʼ ₂ⲛ̅ˑ ₂ⲛ̅ [ⲧⲙⲛⲧⲣ̅ⲣⲟ ⲙ̅ⲡⲉⲭ̅ⲥ̅

20 ⲛ̅ˑⲑⲉˑ ⲛ̅ˑⲛ̣ⲉ̣[ⲛ]ⲧ̣ⲁⲩˑ₂̣[ⲩⲡⲟⲙⲓⲛⲉ ⲛⲉⲛⲧⲁⲩ

₂ⲩⲡⲟˑⲙⲓˑⲛⲉ ⲇⲉʼ ⲡ[ⲉϫⲁϥ ⲛ̅ϭⲓ ⲡⲭⲟⲉⲓⲥ

ϫⲉ] ϯˑⲛⲁˑⲧⲁ̣[ⲁⲥ ⲛⲁⲩ ⲁⲧⲣⲉⲩ₂ⲙⲟⲟⲥ ₂ⲓ

[ⲟⲩⲛⲁⲙ ⲙ̅ⲙⲟ̈ⲓ ⲥⲉⲛⲁⲭⲣⲟ ⲉⲡϣⲏⲣⲉ ⲛ̅ⲧⲁⲛⲟ]

13 ⲛ̅ⲟⲩⲁ ⲛⲟⲩⲁ Sa³*ᵛⁱᵈ | 15 ⲙ̅ⲛ̅ Sa³* |

1 ⲉ₂ⲣⲁ̈ⲓ Sa³ᵛⁱᵈ = Ach: om Sa¹ | 2-3 ⲉⲣⲉ - ⲉⲣⲟⲟⲩ Sa³ Sa¹ (ⲉ-...
ϥⲛⲁⲛⲁⲩ...): ⲉⲡⲗⲗⲟⲥ ⲧⲏⲣϥ ⲛⲟ ⲁⲣⲁⲩ ⲙ̅ⲛ ⲡⲕⲟⲥⲙⲟⲥ ⲧⲏⲣϥ Ach | 3
ⲛ̅ϥ̅ⲧ̅ⲙ̅ϣ̅ϭ̅ⲙ̅ϭⲟⲙ Sa³ = Sa¹: ϥⲛⲁϭⲛ̅ϭⲁⲙ... ⲉⲛ Ach | 4 ϥⲛⲁϭⲱⲛⲧ Sa³
Sa¹: ϥⲛⲁⲃⲱⲕ Ach | ⲁⲩⲱ Sa³: om Sa¹ Ach | 4-5 ϥⲛⲁⲕⲱⲧⲉ Sa³
Sa¹: ϥϣⲓⲛⲉ Ach | 5-6 ϥⲛⲁⲕⲉⲗⲉⲩⲉ ⲛ̅ⲥⲉⲣⲱⲕ₂ Sa³ = Sa¹: ϥⲛⲁⲡⲱⲧ
ⲥⲉⲛⲉⲧⲟⲩⲁⲁⲃⲉ ⲧⲏⲣⲟⲩ ⲥⲉⲛⲧⲟⲩ ⲉⲩⲙⲏⲣ ⲙ̅ⲛ ⲛ̅ⲟⲩⲓ̈ⲉⲓⲃⲉ ⲙ̅ⲡⲕⲁ₂ ϥⲛⲁ₂ⲱⲧⲃⲉ
ⲙ̅ⲙⲁⲩ ϥⲣⲟⲗⲓⲕⲉ ⲙ̅ⲙⲁⲩ [1 line lacuna] ⲙ̅ⲙⲁⲩ ⲥⲉⲉⲓⲛⲉ Ach | 6
ⲛ̅ⲛⲉⲩⲃⲁⲗ Sa³ = Sa¹: + ⲁⲃⲁⲗ Ach | ⲟⲩϭⲁ₂ Sa³ = Sa¹: ₂ⲉⲛϣⲗⲓϭ Ach
| 7 ϥⲛⲁⲉⲓⲛⲉ Sa³: pr ϥⲛⲁⲛⲛⲉⲩϣⲗⲁⲣ ⲉⲃⲟⲗ ⲛ̅ⲧⲉⲩⲁⲡⲉ Sa¹: pr ϥⲛⲁⲉⲓⲛⲉ
ⲛ̅ⲟⲩⲉⲁⲁⲣⲉ ⲁⲃⲁⲗ ₂ⲛ̅ⲛ ⲟⲩⲁⲡⲏⲩⲉ Ach | 8 ⲛ̅ⲥⲉⲛⲉⲭ Sa³ Sa¹: ⲥⲉϯ Ach
| 8-9 ₂ⲓⲕⲟⲛⲓⲁ - ⲉϣⲁⲛⲧⲟⲩ Sa³ Sa¹: ⲁϥϭⲉⲛⲧⲟⲩ ₂ⲓⲕⲟⲛⲓⲁ Ach | 9
ⲛⲏ Sa³: ⲛⲁ̈ⲓ Sa¹ = Ach | 9-10 ⲉⲧⲉⲙ̅ⲡⲟⲩϣ ⲧⲱⲟⲩⲛ Sa³ = Ach:
ⲥⲉⲛⲁϣϥⲓ ⲉⲛ Sa¹ | 11 ⲛ̅ⲛⲉⲩⲛⲟⲩⲃ Sa³ = Sa¹: ⲛ̅ⲛⲟⲩⲃ Ach | ₂ⲓⲭⲛ̅
Sa³ Ach: ⲉ₂ⲣⲁ̈ⲓ ⲉϫⲛ̅ Sa¹ | 12 ⲉⲩⲭⲱ - ϫⲓⲟⲣ Sa³ = Sa¹: om Ach |
ⲙ̅ⲙⲟⲛ ⲉⲧⲉⲣⲏⲙⲟⲥ Sa³ = Sa¹: ⲁ₂ⲉⲛⲙⲁ ⲛ̅ⲉⲣⲏⲙⲟⲥ Ach | 14 ⲉⲣⲉ ...
ⲛⲁϣⲉⲡ Sa³: ⲛⲁϣⲱⲡ Sa¹ Ach | ⲛⲉⲩⲡ̅ⲛ̅ⲁ̅ Sa³ = Ach: ⲡⲉⲡ̅ⲛ̅ⲁ̅ Sa¹ |

[17]

that time they will raise cries of joy towards

heaven, shining forth as the whole world watches

them. The lawless one will not prevail

against them. He will become angry with the land and

5   try to sin against the people. He will command

that their eyes be burnt out with an iron

rod. He will tear off their nails one by one.

He will command that vinegar and lye be poured

into their nostrils. And those who are unable to

10   endure that king's tortures will

take their gold and flee by the ferries

saying, "Ferry us across to the desert."

They will pass away like one asleep,

as the Lord takes to himself their spirits and

15   their souls. Their flesh will be like

ham. No wild animal will eat them until

the final day of the great judgement. They

will rise and receive a place of rest, but

they will not be part of the kingdom of the Christ

20   like those who endured. "But as for those

who endured," says the Lord,

"I will direct them to sit on

my right." They will be victorious over the lawless

| 15 ΝΕΥΨΥΧΗ Sa³ = Ach: ΝΕΨΥΧΟΟΥΕ Sa¹ | 15-16 ΝΛϢϢΠΕ (ΤϢΠΕ
Sa¹) ϢΟΘ ΝΝΙΠΕΡΝΛ Sa³ᵛⁱᵈ Sa¹: ΝΛϨϢΠΕ ΕΥΕ ΝΠΕΤΡΛ Ach | 17
ΚΡΙϹΙϹ Sa³ Sa¹: + ΛΟΥ Ach | 17-18 ϹΕΝΛΤϢΟΥΝΟΥ Sa³: ϹΕΝΛΤϢΟΥΝ
Sa¹ = Ach | 18 ΝϹΕΧΙ Sa³ Sa¹ (ϹΕΧΙ): ϹΕϬΙΝΕ Ach | ΝΟΥΜΛ
ΝΜΤΟΝ Sa³ = Ach: ΝΟΥΝΤΟΝ Sa¹ | 19 ϹΕΝΛϢϢΠΕ – ΠΕⲬⲤ Sa³ⁱⁿᶜ =
Ach(om ϨΝ): ϹΕϢΕΙ ΝΟΥΝΤΟΝ ϢϢΠΕ ΜΝ ΠΕⲬⲤ Sa¹ | 20-21
ΝΕΝΤΛΥϨΥΠΟΜΙΝΕ ΛΕ Sa³: om Sa¹ Ach | 22 ϮΝΛΤΛΛϹ Sa³ᵛⁱᵈ = Ach:
ϮΝΛΤΛϹϹΕ Sa¹ | 23 ΝΜΟΪ Sa³ⁱⁿᶜ = Sa¹: ΝΜΛΥ Ach | ϹΕΝΛⳬΡΟ
Sa³ᵛⁱᵈ Sa¹: pr ϹΕΝΛΧΙ ϨΜΛΤ ΛΧΝ ϨΕΝΚΕΚΕΥΕ Ach |

‾IH‾

м·еі[λ]

с]е̣н̣[λνλγ ен]вωλ·   ев[ολ Ν̄тп]е̣ мη̣ [пκλ2

с̣[енλхι]   η̣λι·ѳро·η̣[ос]   м̄·пе·о·оγ′   м̄η̣   [некλ

ом′   се·н[λс]ωт̄м   η̄·6ι·   ϭ̄мт·хоγ·ωт·   ν̄·λ̣[ι]κλ[ι

ос′   2̄ν·   н[е]2о·оγ·   е·т̄м·мλγ′   νλ·ϊ·   ет·с̄в·тω[т

5   е·теγ·н[оγ]   се·νλ·2о·коγ·   2̄м·   фωк·   м̄·пноγ·т[е

с̣енλп[ω]т̣′   е·2рλ·ϊ′   е·ѳι·е·роγ·сλ·λнм′   еγ·м[ι

ϣе·   м̄ν·   [п]λ̣т̣·ϣι·пе·   еγ·хω·   м̄·мос·   хе·   6о[м

нιм·   ентλ·не·про·ф[нтн]с·   λ·λγ·   λ·к[λλγ]   λλλ[

м̄пек·ϣ·6м̄·6ом·   [νλ]м̣е   е·тоγ·не[с]   о̣γ̣р̣еϥ·

10   мо·оγт′   е·вол·   хе·   м̄[ν]   6̣ом·   м̄·м[о]к′   2̄м·   пλ·ϊ

λν·с̣оγω̄ν̣т̣   хе·   [ν̄то]к·   пе·   пϣн·ре·   ν̄·тλ·νо·

мι·λ·   ϥνλ·сω·т̣[м̄   ν̄]6ι   пλ·т·ϣ[ι]пе′   [ν̄]ϥ·6онт·[

ν̄ϥκελ]еγ·е′   ν̄·с[емо]γр·   ν̄·ν̄·λικ[λιос   ν̄се

тλλγ   е2р[λ̣]ϊ′   еη̣[ϣ]н̣оγ̣·е   ν̄·се·рωκ[2]   м̣м[ооγ

15   λγω   2̄м]   пе·2о·оγ   е·т̄м·мλγ′   фнт   ν̄·νоγ[

мннϣе]·   νλ·пωϣс′   е·ро·оγ′   ν̄·сесλ·2ω·о̣[γ

евол   м̄моϥ′   е]γ·хω·   м̄·мос′   хе·   пλ·ϊ·   λν·   пе[

пех̄с̄   мн   ер]е̣·   пе·х̣[с̄]·   ν̄·гλр·   2ω·т̄в·   λ̣![

κλιос   ме]ϥ·пωт̣   ν̄·с̣λ·   р̄м·м̄·ме′   ϥνλ̣[

20   кωте   λν   ν̄сλ   м̄п]еι·ѳе·   м̄·мо·оγ′   2̄ν·   2ен[

мλеιν   м̄ν   2енϣпн]·р̣[е]   2̄м·   пе·2о·оγ·   е̣[

т̄ммλγ   пехрιстос   ν]λ̣·ϣ̄ν̄2̣   2т̄ηϥ

---

2 νλιѳроνос (= νε-?) Sa³ Sa¹ (ν̄ѳр.): ν̄ν̄ѳроνос Ach | 3
сенλсωт̄м Sa³ = Ach: сенλсωтп Sa¹ | ν̄6ι Sa³ = Ach: om Sa¹ |
4 2̄ν νε2ооγ ет̄ммλγ Sa³ = Sa¹: om Ach | 5 2̄м- Sa³ = Sa¹: м̄-
Ach | 6 сенλпωт Sa³ Sa¹: сепωт Ach | е2рλ̣ϊ Sa³: om Sa¹ Ach
| 6-7 еγмϣе Sa³ = Ach: еγполемι Sa¹ | 7 м̄ν Sa³ Ach: ν̄мλγ
λγω Sa¹ | 8 ентλ- Sa³: етλ... Sa¹ Ach | λλγ Sa³ Sa¹: +
хν̄ ν̄2λрп Ach | λλλ Sa³: om Sa¹ Ach | 9 м̄пек6м̄6ом Sa³ = Ach:
м̄пек6м̄6ом Sa¹ | νλме Sa³vid: om Sa¹ Ach | 10 м̄мок Sa³ Sa¹: +
λ†ѱγхн Ach | 12 ν̄6ι пλтϣιпе Sa³ = Sa¹: om Ach | ν̄ϥ6онт Sa³ =
Sa¹: ϥвωλк Ach | 13 ν̄ϥκελеγе Sa³ = Sa¹: + λхеро ν̄2еν2нγе
Ach | ν̄ν̄λικλιос Sa³ Ach: ν̄λικλιос Sa¹ | 14 енϣноγе Sa³ Sa¹:
om Ach | 15 λγω Sa³vid = Ach: om Sa¹ | 15-16 ν̄νоγмннϣе Sa³vid=
Sa¹: ν̄2λ2 Ach | 16 νλпωϣс Sa³ Sa¹: νλν̄2λт Ach | ν̄сесλ2ϣоγ
Sa³ = Sa¹: сепωт Ach | 17 пλϊ Sa³ = Ach: pr м̄ Sa¹ | 18 мн ер·
Sa³vid = Sa¹: мλ Ach | ν̄гλр Sa³: om Sa¹ Ach | 19 р̄м̄ме Sa³ =
Sa¹: рωме Ach | 19-20 ϥνλкωте - ν̄сλ м̄- Sa³vid: мн еϥкωте ν̄тоϥ
ен ν̄2оγо ν̄сλ м̄- Sa¹: еϥνλϣιне λλλ λ2λреϥр̄-Ach | 21 2̄м
пе2ооγ Sa³ = Sa¹: 2̄ν ν̄2ооγе Ach |

[18]

one. They will see the destruction of heaven and earth.

They will receive the thrones of glory and the crowns.

Sixty righteous ones, prepared for that moment,

will hear at that time.

5   They will don the armour of God.

They will hasten to Jerusalem in their battle

with the shameless one, saying, "Every feat

which the prophets performed, you have performed, but

you were in truth unable to raise a

10 dead person, because you lack the power. By this

did we recognize you as the lawless

one." The shameless one will hear, become angry

and command that the righteous be bound,

be placed on altars and be burnt.

15 And at that time they will win

the affection of many. They will

leave him, saying, "This one is not

the Christ, for the Christ does not kill

righteous people nor does he pursue men. He will

20 not try to convince them by

signs and wonders." At that time

the Christ will have compassion

→ [ιθ]

ⲍⲁ ⲛⲉⲧⲉ ⲛⲟⲩϥ ⲛⲉ] ϥⲛ[ⲁⲧ]ⲛ̄·ⲛ[ⲟⲟⲩ ⲛ̄ⲛⲉ]ϥ
ⲁⲅⲅⲉⲗⲟⲥ] ⲉⲃⲟⲗ· ⲍ̄ⲛ ⲧⲡ[ⲉ]′ [ⲉ]ⲩ·ⲙⲉⲍⲥ̣[ⲟⲟⲩ] ⲛ̄·ⲧⲃⲁ·
ⲙ̄ⲛ ϥⲧⲟ̣·ⲟⲩ· ⲛ̄·ϣⲟ′ ⲉⲟⲩ[ⲛ ⲥⲟⲟⲩ] ⲛ̄·ⲧ̄ⲛ[ⲍ] ⲙ̄·ⲡⲟⲩⲁ·
ⲡⲟⲩⲁ]· ⲙⲟ·ⲟⲩ· ⲡⲉⲩ·ⲍⲣⲟ·ⲟ̣[ⲩ ⲛⲁ]ⲕⲓⲙ· ⲉ·ⲧ[ⲡⲉ] ⲙ̄ⲛ·
5 ⲡⲕⲁⲍ ⲉ]ⲩ·ⲥⲙⲟⲩ· ⲁⲩ·ⲱ· ⲉⲩ[† ⲉⲟ]ⲟⲩ′ ⲛⲁⲓ̣ ⲉ̣[ⲧ]ⲉ̣ⲣⲉ̣·
ⲡⲣⲁⲛ] ⲙ̄·ⲡⲉ·ⲭⲥ̄· ⲥⲏⲍ· [ⲉⲝ]ⲛ̣ ⲧⲉⲩⲧⲉⲍ[ⲛⲉ ⲉⲣⲉ
ⲧⲉⲥϲⲣⲁ]·ⲅⲓⲥ· ⲍⲓ·ⲭⲛ̄· ⲧⲉ̣[ⲩ]ϭⲓⲝ· ⲛ̄·ⲛⲟⲩ·ⲛⲁⲙ [ⲭⲓ
ⲛⲟⲩⲕⲟⲩⲓ]· ϣⲁ· ⲟⲩ·ⲛⲟ[ϭ ⲥ]ⲉ·ⲛⲁ·ⲧⲁ·ⲗⲟ·ⲟⲩ′
ⲉⲭ̄ⲛ ⲛⲟⲩⲧ[ⲛ̄ⲍ ⲛ̄·ⲥⲉ·ϥⲓ[ⲧⲟⲩ]· ⲍⲁ·ⲑⲏ· ⲙ̄·ⲡϭⲱⲛⲧ′[
10 ⲧⲟⲧⲉ ⲅⲁⲃⲣ]ⲓ̣·ⲏⲗ′ ⲙ̄ⲛ· ⲟ[ⲩⲣⲓ]·ⲏⲗ′ ⲥⲉ·ⲛⲁ·ⲣ̄ ⲟⲩ·
ⲥⲧⲩⲗ[ⲟⲥ ⲛ̄]·ⲟⲩ·ⲟ·ⲉⲓⲛ′ [ⲛ̄]ⲥ̣ⲉ̣·ⲥⲱⲕ· ⲍⲁ· ⲧⲉⲩ·ⲍⲏ·[
ϣⲁⲛ[ⲧⲟⲩⲭⲓ]ⲧ̣ⲟⲩ′ ⲉ·ⲍⲟⲩⲛ′ ⲉ·ⲡⲕⲁⲍ· ⲉ·ⲧⲟⲩ·ⲁ·ⲁⲃ·[
ⲛ̄·ⲥⲉ[ⲧⲁⲁ]ⲥ ⲛ̄[ⲁⲩ ⲉ]ⲧ̣ⲣⲉⲩ·ⲟⲩ·ⲱⲙ· ⲉ·ⲃⲟⲗ̣· ⲍ̄ⲙ·[
ⲡϣⲏ[ⲛ ⲙ̄]ⲡ[ⲱⲛⲍ] ⲛ̄·ⲥⲉ·ϥ[ⲟ]·ⲣⲓ′ ⲛ̄ⲧ̄· ⲍ̄ⲃⲥ[ⲱ ⲛ̄
15 ⲟⲩ·ⲱⲃ̣[ϣ] ⲛ̄ⲥⲉ[ⲣⲟⲉⲓ]ⲥ′ ⲉ·ⲣⲟ·ⲟⲩ· ⲛ̄·ϭⲓ· ⲛⲁⲅⲅ̣[ⲉⲗⲟⲥ
ⲛ̄ⲥⲉ·[ⲛ̄]ⲁ̣·ⲍ̣[ⲕⲟ ⲁ]ⲛ̣ [ⲟ]ⲩ·ⲗⲉ· ⲛ̄·ⲥⲉ·ⲛⲁ·ⲉⲓ[ⲃⲉ ⲁⲛ ⲟⲩ
ⲁ̣[ⲉ ϥⲛⲁϭⲙ̄ϭⲟⲙ ⲉ]ⲣⲟ·ⲟⲩ· ⲁⲛ′ ⲛ̄·ⲉ̣ⲓ· [ⲡϣⲏⲣⲉ ⲛ̄
ⲧⲁⲛⲟⲙⲓⲁ ⲍ̄ⲙ ⲡⲉ]ⲍⲟ·ⲟⲩ· ⲁⲉ· [ⲉⲧⲙ̄ⲙⲁⲩ ⲡⲕⲁⲍ
ⲧⲏ]ⲣ̣ϥ ⲛ̄[ⲁϣⲧⲟⲣⲧ̄ⲣ̄′ ⲡⲣⲏ· ⲛ[ⲁⲣ̄ ⲕⲁⲕⲉ] ⲥⲉ[
20 ⲛⲁ]ϥⲓ· ⲛ̄[†ⲣⲏⲛⲏ]′ ⲍⲓ·ⲭⲙ̄ [ⲡⲕⲁⲍ ⲁⲩⲱ] ⲍⲁ ⲧⲡⲉ[
...] . [........] . ′ . [........] . [..]
.... ⲛ̄]ϣⲏⲛ· ⲥ̣[ⲉⲛⲁⲡⲱⲣⲕ ⲛ̄ⲥⲉⲍⲉ
ⲛ̄ⲑⲏⲣⲓⲟⲛ ⲙ̄ⲛ ⲛ̄]·ⲧ̄ⲃ·ⲛⲟ̣[ⲟⲩⲉ ⲥⲉⲛⲁⲙⲟⲩ ⲍ̄ⲛ ⲟⲩ
ϣⲧⲟⲣⲧ̄ⲣ̄ ⲛ̄ⲍⲁⲗⲉⲧⲉ]′ ⲛⲁ·ⲍ̣ⲉ· [ⲉⲭ̄ⲙ ⲡⲕⲁⲍ ⲉⲩⲙⲟ

---

20 ⲍⲁⲡⲉ Sa³* |

1 ϥⲛⲁⲧⲛ̄ⲛⲟⲟⲩ Sa³ = Ach: ⲛ̄ϥⲧⲛ̄ⲛⲟⲟⲩ Sa¹ | 2 ⲍ̄ⲛ Sa³ Sa¹: ⲛ̄ Ach |
4 ⲡⲉⲩⲍⲣⲟⲟⲩ Sa³ Sa¹: ⲡⲁⲣⲁⲩ Ach | 5 ⲁⲩⲱ Sa³ Sa¹: om Ach | ⲛⲁⲓ̈
Sa³ Sa¹: +ⲗⲉ Ach | 6 ⲉⲣⲉ Sa³vid Sa¹: om Ach | 7 ⲛ̄ⲛⲟⲩⲛⲁⲙ Sa³
= Sa¹: om Ach | 8 ⲭⲓⲛ ⲟⲩⲕⲟⲩⲓ ϣⲁ ⲟⲩⲛⲟϭ Sa³vid: ⲭⲛ̄ ⲡⲟⲩⲕⲟⲩⲉⲓ ϣⲁ
ⲡⲟⲩⲛⲟϭ Sa¹: ⲛⲓⲍⲏⲙ ⲙ̄ⲛ ⲛⲓⲛⲁϭ Ach | 9 ⲉⲭ̄ⲛ Sa³vid = Ach: ⲡⲣ
ⲉⲍⲣⲁ̈ⲓ Sa¹ | ⲍⲁⲑⲏ ⲙ̄ⲡϭⲱⲛⲧ Sa³ = Sa¹: ⲍⲓⲧⲍⲓ ⲛ̄ⲧϥⲃ̄ⲕⲉ Ach |
10-11 ⲥⲉⲛⲁⲣ̄ ⲟⲩⲥⲧⲩⲗⲟⲥ Sa³ Sa¹: ⲛⲁⲣ̄ ⲥⲧⲩⲗⲟⲥ Ach | 11 ⲛ̄ⲥⲉⲥⲱⲕ
Sa³ = Sa¹: ⲉⲩⲥⲱⲕ Ach | ⲍⲁ ⲧⲉⲩⲍⲏ Sa³ Sa¹: ⲍⲛ̄ⲧⲟⲩ Ach | 12
ϣⲁⲛⲧⲟⲩⲭⲓⲧⲟⲩ Sa³ Sa¹: om Ach | ⲉⲡⲕⲁⲍ Sa³ = Ach: ⲉⲙ̄ⲡⲙⲁ Sa¹ | 13
ⲛ̄ⲥⲉⲧⲁⲁⲥ Sa³vid = Ach: ⲥⲉⲧⲁⲥⲥⲉ Sa¹ | 16 ⲛ̄ⲥⲉⲛⲁⲍⲕⲟ - ⲟⲩⲗⲉ Sa³
Sa¹ (ⲥⲉⲛⲁⲍⲕⲟ): om Achvid | ⲛ̄ⲥⲉⲛⲁⲉⲓⲃⲉ Sa³: ⲥⲉⲛⲁⲉⲓⲃⲉ Sa¹ |
17-18 ϥⲛⲁϭⲙ̄ϭⲟⲙ - ⲛ̄ⲧⲁⲛⲟⲙⲓⲁ Sa³: ⲡϣⲏⲣⲉ ⲛ̄ⲧⲁⲛⲟⲙⲓⲁ ⲛⲁϭⲙ̄ϭⲟⲙ ⲉⲣⲟⲟⲩ
ⲁⲛ Sa¹ = Achvid | 18 ⲗⲉ Sa³: ϭⲉ Sa¹ | 19 ⲧⲏⲣϥ Sa³vid: om Sa¹
Achvid | ⲥⲉⲛⲁϥⲓ ⲛ̄†ⲣⲏⲛⲏ Sa³vid = Achvid: ⲥⲉϥⲓ †ⲣⲏⲛⲏ Sa¹ | 20
ⲍⲁⲧⲡⲉ Sa³vid: ⲡⲉⲡⲛ̄ⲁ Sa¹ |

[19]

on those who are his. He will send his

angels from heaven, sixty-four thousand

in number, each having six

wings. Their voices will move heaven and

5   earth, when they praise and give glory. Those

upon whose forehead is written the name of the Christ,

upon whose right hand is the seal,

both small and great, they will be taken

on their wings and removed from the wrath.

10   Then Gabriel and Uriel will be

a column of light and go before them

until they bring them to the holy land,

and they will permit them to eat from

the tree of life and to wear white

15   garments, while the angels keep watch over them.

They will neither hunger nor thirst, nor

will the lawless one have power

over them. And at that time the whole

earth will tremble. The sun will be darkened. Peace

20   will be removed from upon the earth and from under heaven

. . . .

. . . . the trees will be uprooted and topple.

Wild animals and domestic animals will die in

confusion. Birds will fall on the ground dead

↑   [ᴋ̄]

ογτ λγω]· ⲛ̄·ⲙⲟ[ɣⲉɪ]ⲟ·ⲟ[ɣⲉ ⲛ̄ⲑⲁⲗⲗⲁⲥⲥⲁ

ⲛⲁ·ⲱ[ϣⲙ]· ⲛ̄ⲣ̄·ⲉ[ϥ]ⲣ̄ ⲛⲟ̣ⲃ̣ⲉ̣ [ⲛⲁϣϣ ⲉ₂ⲟⲟⲙ

₂ɪ·ⲭ̄ⲙ ⲡ̣ⲕⲁ₂· [ⲉɣⲭⲱ] ⲙ̄·ⲙⲟⲥ· ⲭⲉ· ⲟɣ ⲡ[ⲉⲧⲁⲕ

ⲗⲗ[ϥ]· ⲛⲁⲛ· ⲡ̣ϣ[ⲏⲣⲉ ⲛ̄·ⲧⲁ·ⲛⲟ·ⲙⲓⲁ· ⲉⲕ[ⲭⲱ ⲙ̄

5 ⲙ[ⲟⲥ· ⲁ·ⲛⲟ̣ⲕ [ⲡⲉ] ⲡ̣ⲉ·ⲭⲥ̄· ⲉⲛ·ⲧⲟⲕ [ⲡ̣ϣⲏⲣⲉ

ⲛ̄ⲧⲁ]·ⲛⲟ·ⲙⲓ·ⲁ· [ⲛ̄ⲧⲟⲕ]· ⲇ̣ⲉ· ⲙ̄·ⲙⲛ̄· ⳓⲟⲙ [ⲙ̄ⲙⲟⲕ

ⲉⲛⲟɣ·₂ⲙ̄ ⲙ̄ⲙⲟⲕ· [ⲭ]ⲉ̣· ⲉⲕⲉ·ⲛⲁ·₂ⲙ̣ⲧ̣ⲛ̄ ⲁⲕⲣ̄ ₂ⲛ̄

ⲙⲁ·ⲉⲓⲛ· ⲉɣ·ϣⲟɣ·ⲉ̣[ⲓⲧ]· ⲛ̄·ⲡⲉⲛ·ⲛ̄ⲙ[ⲧⲟ ⲉⲃⲟⲗ ϣⲁⲛ

ⲧ̄ⲕ·ⲁ·ⲁⲛ· ⲛ̄·ϣⲙ̄·ⲙ̣[ⲟ]· ⲉ·ⲡⲉ·ⲭⲥ̄· ⲡ[ⲉⲧⲁϥⲧⲁ

10 ⲙⲓ·ⲟ· ⲛ̄·ⲟɣ·ⲟⲛ· ⲛⲓ̣ⲙ [ⲟ]ɣ·ⲟⲉⲓ· ⲛⲁⲛ· ⳽[ⲉ ⲁⲛⲥⲱⲧ]ⲙ̣̄[

ⲛ̄·ⲥⲱⲕ· ⲉⲓⲥ· ₂ⲏ·ⲏⲧ̣ⲉ̣· ⲁ·ⲛⲟⲛ· ⲧⲉ[ⲛⲟɣ ⲉ]ⲛ̣ⲁ·ⲙⲟɣ· [

₂ⲛ̄·ⲛ ⲟɣ·₂ⲉ· ⲃⲱ·ⲱⲛ· ⲙ̄ⲛ̄·ⲛ ⲟɣ·ⲑ[ⲗ]ⲓ̣ⲯ[ⲓⲥ ⲉⲥⲧ]ϣⲛ· ⳓⲉ·

ⲧⲉ·ⲛⲟɣ· ⲧⲁⳓ·ⲥⲉ· ⲛ̄·ⲟ[ɣⲁⲓⲕⲁⲓ]ⲟ̣ⲥ [ⲛ̄ⲧⲛ̄]ⲟɣⲱ[

ϣ]ⲧ̣ ⲙ̄·ⲙⲟⲅ· ⲏ· ⲉϥ·ⲧⲱⲛ· [ⲡⲉ] ⳨·ⲥ̣[ⲃ]ϣ· ⲛⲁ̣ⲛ·

15 ⲛ̄ⲧⲛ̄·ⲡⲁ·ⲣⲁ·ⲕⲁ·ⲗⲉⲓ· ⲙ̄·ⲙ[ⲟϥ ⲧ]ⲉⲛ̣ⲟ[ɣ] ⳓⲉ· ⲉⲛ·

ⲁⲧⲁ]·ⲕⲟ· ₂ⲛ̄· ⲟɣ·ⲟⲣ·ⲅⲏ· ⲭⲉ· [ⲁⲛⲣ̄ ⲁⲧⲥⲱ]ⲧ̣ⲙ̄· ⲛ̄·

ⲥⲁ ⲡⲛⲟ]ɣ·ⲧⲉ· ⲁⲛ·ⲃⲱⲕ· ⲉ[ⲛ̄ⲙⲁ ⲉⲧϣⲏⲕ ₂ⲛ̄

ⲑⲁⲗⲗⲁⲥⲥⲁ] ⲙ̄·ⲡⲉⲛ·ⳓⲙ [ⲙⲟⲟɣ ⲁⲛϣⲓⲕⲉ

₂ⲛ̄ ⲉⲓⲣ̄ϣⲟɣ ⲙ]ⲛ̄·ⲛⲁ·ⲥⲉ [ⲙ̄ⲙⲁ₂]ⲉ· ⲙ̄[ⲡⲉⲛⳓⲙ

20 ⲙⲟⲟɣ ⲁⲛ ⲧⲟ]·ⲧⲉ· ϥⲛ̣[ⲁⲣⲓⲙⲉ ⲛ̄]·ⳓⲓ· [ⲡⲁⲧϣⲓⲡⲉ

..........] ... [..............]· [₂ⲙ̄

ⲡⲉ₂ⲟⲟɣ ⲉⲧⲙ̄]ⲙⲁɣ ⲉ[ϥⲭⲱ ⲙ̄ⲙⲟⲥ ⲭⲉ

ⲟɣⲟⲉⲓ ⲛⲁⲓ̈ ₂]ⲱ· ⲭⲉ· ⲁ[ⲡⲁⲟɣⲟⲉⲓϣ ⲟɣ

ⲉⲓⲛⲉ ⲉⲣⲟⲓ̈}}]}}}}ⳳ[

---

8 ⲡⲉⲛⲛ̄ⲧⲟ Sa³* | 10 -ⲙⲓⲟⲟ Sa³* | 12 ⲙⲛ Sa³* |

1 ⲁγⲱ Sa³ᵛⁱᵈ: ⲡⲕⲁ₂ ⲛⲁϣⲟⲟɣⲉ ⲁγⲱ Sa¹ = Ach (om ⲁγⲱ) |
ⲛ̄ⲙⲟγⲉⲓⲟⲟγⲉ Sa³ = Ach: ⲙ̄ⲙⲟγ Sa¹ | ⲛ̄ⲑⲁⲗⲗⲁⲥⲥⲁ Sa³ᵛⁱᵈ Ach:
ⲉⲑⲁⲗⲗⲁⲥⲥⲁ Sa¹ | 2 ⲛⲁϣϣⲙ Sa³ Sa¹: ⲛⲁϣⲉγⲉ Ach | 5 ⲭⲉ Sa³ Sa¹:
om Ach | ⲉⲛⲧⲟⲕ Sa³ᵛⁱᵈ Ach: + ⲡⲉ Sa¹ | 5-6 ⲡϣⲏⲣⲉ ⲛ̄ⲧⲁⲛⲟⲙⲓⲁ
Sa³ Sa¹: ⲡⲁⲓⲁⲃⲟⲗⲟⲥ Ach | 6 ⲛ̄ⲧⲟⲕ ⲇⲉ Sa³: om Sa¹ Ach | 7 ⲭⲉ
Sa³ Ach: ⲭⲉⲕⲁⲁⲥ Sa¹ | ⲉⲕⲉⲛⲁ₂ⲙ̄ⲛ Sa³ = Sa¹: ⲕⲛⲁⲛⲁ₂ⲙⲛⲉ Ach |
8 ⲉγϣⲟγⲉⲓⲧ Sa³ Sa¹: om Ach | 9-10 ⲡⲉⲧⲁϥⲧⲁⲙⲓⲟ ⲛ̄ⲟγⲟⲛ ⲛⲓⲙ Sa³:
ⲡⲉⲧⲁϥⲧⲁⲙⲓⲟⲛ Sa¹: ⲉⲧⲁ₂ⲧⲉⲛⲁⲛ Ach | 10 ⲛⲁⲛ Sa³ = Ach: +
ⲉⲛⲟⲛ Sa¹ | 12 ⲙ̄ⲛⲛ ⲟγⲑⲗⲓⲯⲓⲥ Sa³ = Sa¹: om Achᵛⁱᵈ | 14 ⲙ̄ⲙⲟⲅ
Sa³: om Sa¹: ⲙ̄ⲙⲁⲥ Ach | 15-16 ⲉⲛⲁⲧⲁⲕⲟ Sa³ Sa¹: ⲧ̄ⲛ̄ⲛⲁⲧⲉⲕⲟ
Ach | 20 ⲁⲛ Sa³ᵛⁱᵈ: om Sa¹ | ϥⲛⲁⲣⲓⲙⲉ Sa³: ⲁϥⲣⲓⲙⲉ Sa¹ |

[20]

and the waters of the sea

will evaporate. The sinners will cry out

on the earth, saying, "What have you done

to us, lawless one, by saying,

5   'I am the Christ,' when you are the

lawless one? And you have no power

to save yourself, much less to save us. You performed

vain marvels before us until

you had made us strangers to the Christ who

10   created each one of us. Woe to us, because we listened

to you! See, we are about to die

in an evil manner and in affliction. Where

now is the footprint of a righteous person, that we

should worship you, or where is our teacher

15   that we might appeal to him? Now we

will be destroyed by wrath, because we disobeyed

God. We went to the depths of

the sea but found no water. We dug in

the riverbeds sixteen cubits, but failed to

20   find water." Then the shameless one will weep

. . . . at

that time, saying

"Woe is me as well, because my time has

passed!"

Sa[1] 13,23 ⲛⲉⲉⲓⲭⲱ ⲙ̄

ⲙⲟⲥ ϫⲉ ⲛⲁⲟⲩⲟⲉⲓϣ ⲛ̄

25 ⲛⲁⲟⲩⲉⲓⲛⲉ ⲉⲣⲟⲉⲓ ⲁⲛ

ⲁⲛⲛⲁⲣⲟⲙⲡⲉ ϣⲱⲡⲉ

ⲛ̄ⲛⲓⲉⲃⲟⲧ: ⲁⲛⲁⲡⲟⲟⲩⲉ ⲉ

ⲧⲃ̄ ⲛ̄ⲑⲉ ⲛ̄ⲛⲓϣⲟⲉⲓϣ ⲉϣ

ϣⲁϥⲟⲩⲱⲧⲃ̄: ⲧⲉⲛⲟⲩ ϭⲉ

30 ⲉⲉⲓⲛⲁⲧⲁϭⲟ ⲛ̄ⲙ̄ⲙⲏⲧⲛ̄

ⲧⲉⲛⲟⲩ ϭⲉ ⲡⲱⲧ ⲉⲃⲟⲗ ⲉ

ⲧⲉⲣⲏⲙⲟⲥ: ϭⲉⲡ ⲛⲓⲥⲟⲟ

ⲛⲉ ⲍⲱⲧⲃ̄ ⲙ̄ⲙⲟⲟⲩ:

ⲁⲛⲉⲧⲟⲩⲁⲁⲃ ⲁⲛⲓⲥⲟⲩ ⲁⲍ

35 ⲍⲣⲁ̈ⲓ ⲉⲧⲃⲏⲧⲟⲩ ⲅⲁⲣ ⲉⲣⲉ

14,1 ⲡⲕⲁⲍ {ⲉⲣⲉ ⲡⲕⲁⲍ} † ⲕⲁⲣⲡⲟⲥ

ⲉⲧⲃⲏⲧⲟⲩ ⲅⲁⲣ ⲉⲣⲉ ⲡⲣⲏ ⲣ̄

ⲟⲩⲟⲉⲓⲛ ⲉⲍⲣⲁ̈ⲓ ⲉϫⲙ̄ ⲡⲕⲁⲍ

ⲉⲧⲃⲏⲧⲟⲩ ⲅⲁⲣ ⲉⲣⲉ †ⲱⲧⲉ

5 ⲛⲏⲟⲩ ⲉϫⲙ̄ ⲡⲕⲁⲍ ⲥⲉⲛⲁ

ⲣⲓⲙⲉ ⲛ̄ϭⲓ ⲛ̄ⲣⲉϥⲣ̄ ⲛⲟⲃⲉ

ⲉⲩϫⲱ ⲙ̄ⲙⲟⲥ ϫⲉ ⲁⲕⲁⲁ̤ⲛ

ⲛ̄ϫⲁϫⲉ ⲁⲡⲛⲟⲩⲧⲉ ⲉ[ϣⲱⲡⲉ

ⲟⲩⲛ ϭⲟⲙ {ϭⲟⲙ} ⲙ̄ⲙⲟⲕ [ⲧⲱ

10 ⲟⲩⲛ ⲛ̄ⲅⲡⲱⲧ ⲛ̄ⲥⲱ[ⲟⲩ

ⲧⲟⲧⲉ ϥⲛⲁϫⲓ ⲛ̄ⲛⲉϥⲛ̄ⲧ

ⲛ̄ⲍ ⲛ̄ⲕⲱⲍⲧ ⲛ̄ϥⲍⲱⲗ ⲉⲃⲟⲗ

ⲍⲓ ⲡⲁⲍⲟⲩ ⲛ̄ⲛⲉⲧⲟⲩⲁⲁⲃ

ϥⲛⲁⲡⲟⲗⲉⲙⲓ ⲛ̄ⲙⲁⲩ ⲟⲛ

15 ⲥⲉⲛⲁⲥⲱⲧⲙ̄ ⲛ̄ϭⲓ ⲁⲅⲅⲉⲗⲟⲥ

ⲥⲉⲉⲓ ⲉⲡⲉⲥⲏⲧ ⲥⲉⲡⲟⲗⲉ

ⲙⲓ ⲛ̄ⲙⲁϥ ⲉⲩⲡⲟⲗⲉⲙⲟⲥ

ⲛ̄ⲥⲛϥⲉ ⲉⲩⲟϣ ⲥⲛⲁϣⲱ

ⲡⲉ ⲍⲙ̄ ⲡⲉⲍⲟⲟⲩⲉ ⲉⲧⲙ̄ⲙⲁⲩ

20 ϥⲛⲁⲥⲱⲧⲙ̄ ⲛ̄ϭⲓ ⲡϫⲟⲉⲓⲥ

ⲛ̄ϥⲕⲉⲗⲉⲩⲉ ⲍⲛ̄ ⲟⲩⲛⲟϭ ⲛ̄

ϭⲱⲛ̄ⲧ: ⲛ̄ⲧⲡⲉ ⲙⲛ̄ ⲡⲕⲁⲍ

ⲥⲉⲛⲁⲧⲉⲟⲩⲉ ϭⲱⲍⲧ ⲉⲃⲟⲗ

ⲉⲍⲣⲁ̈ⲓ ⲁⲩⲱ ⲡⲕⲱⲍⲧ ⲛⲁⲉ

Sa¹ 13,23   I said,

"My time

25   shall not pass away.

My years have become

months. My days have

passed like dust that

passes by. Indeed now

30   I shall perish with you!

Now then hasten to

the desert. Seize the brigands

and kill them.

Fetch the saints

35   for on their account does

14.1   the earth give produce;

for on their account does the sun

shine upon the earth;

for on their account does the dew

5   settle on the ground." The sinners

will weep

saying, "You have made us

enemies of God. If you

have the power arise

10   and pursue them!"

Then he will spread his fiery

wings and fly away

in pursuit of the saints

He will again wage war on them.

15   The angels will hear,

come down and wage war

against him, a war

of many swords.

At that time

20   the Lord will hear

and command in great

anger that heaven and earth

spew forth fire.

And the fire will

25 ΜΑϩΤε ϩιϫΜ ΠΚΑϩ Ν̄ϢϤ
Ϥε ϹΝΟΟΥϹ Μ̄ΜΑϩε: Ϥ̄
ΝΑΟΥΩΜ Ν̄ϹΑ Ν̄ΡεϤϤΡ
ΝΟΒε ΜΝ̄ Ν̄ΑΙΑΒΟΛΟϹ:
Ν̄θε Ν̄ΟΥΡΗïΟΥε ΟΥΝ

30 ΟΥϩΑΠ ΟΥΜΗε ΝΑϢΩΠε
ϩΜ̄ Πεϩ ΟΟΥ ετΜ̄ΜΑΥ
Ν̄ΤΟΥεΙ Μ̄ΠΚΑϩ ΝΑ† Μ̄
ΠεΥϩΡΟΟΥ: ϩΜ̄ Πεϩ ΟΟΥε

Ach 41,1 (ΟΥε ϩΜ ϩεΠ Μ̄ΜΙε ϩΜ̄ ϕΟΟΥε ετΜ̄
ΜΟ Ν̄ΤΟΥïεΥε ΜΝ̄ ΠΚΑϩ ΝΑ† Ν̄
ΟΥϩΡΑΥ Ν̄ϩΟΟΥ) ΝΑϢεϫε ΜΝ̄ ΝΟΥ
εΡΗΥ ϫε ΝεΑΤετΝ̄ϹΩΤΜε Μ̄ΠΟΟΥ

5 ε ΑΤϹΜΙ Ν̄ΡΩΜε εϤΜΑϩϩε εΜ
ΠϤεΙ ΑΤΚΡΙϹΙϹ Μ̄ΠϢΗΡε Μ̄ΠΝΟΥ
Τε Ν̄ΝΑΒε Μ̄ΠΟΥε ΠΟΥε ΝΑΩϩε
ΑΡετΟΥ ΑΡΑϤ ϩΜ̄ ΠΜΑ ετΑΥεΟΥε
Μ̄ΜΟ εΙΤε ΝΑϕΟΟΥε εΙΤε ΝΑΤΟΥ

10 ϩΙ ΝΑΔΙΚΑΙΟϹ Ν̄ΤΑΥ ΜΝ̄ ΝΑ.. Π
ϹεΝΑΝΟ ΑΝΡεϤϤ̄ ΝΑΒε ϩΝ Ν[ΟΥ]Κ[Ο]
ΛΑϹΙϹ ΜΝ̄ ΝετΑΥϤ̄ ΑΙΩΚε Μ̄Μ̄[Α]Υ
ΜΝ̄ ΝετΑϩϤ̄ ΠΑΡΑΔΙΔΟΥ ΜΜ[ΑΥ] ϩ
ΠΜΟΥ ΤΟΤε Ν̄ΡεϤϤ̄ ΝΑΒε ϩ..Ọ.

15 .Ḥ ϹεΝΑΝΟ ΑΠΜΑ Ν̄Ν̄ΑΙΚ[ΑΙ]ΟϹ
ΛΟΥ †ϩε ΟΥΝ̄ ΟΥϩΜΑΤ ΝΑϩϢ[Πε]
ϩΝ̄ Ν̄ϩΟΟΥε ετΜ̄ΜΟ ΠετΕ Ν[ΑΙΚΑΙ]

42,1 ΟϹ ΝΑϤ̄ ΑΙΤεΙ Μ̄ΜΑϤ Ν̄ϩΑϩ Ν̄ϹΑΠ
ϹεΝΑΤεεϤ ΝεΥ ϩΜ ϕΟΟΥε ετΜ̄
ΜΟ ΠϪΑεΙϹ ΝΑϤ̄ ΚΡΙΝε Ν̄ΤΠε
ΜΝ̄ ΠΚΑϩ ϤΝΑϤ̄ ΚΡΙΝε Ν̄Νε

5 ΤΑΥϤ̄ ΠΑΡΑΒΑ ϩΝ̄ ΤΠε ΜΝ̄ ΝετΑ
ϩεΙΡε ϩΙϫΜ̄ ΠΚΑϩ ϤΝΑϤ̄ ΚΡΙΝε
Ν̄ΝϢΩϹ Μ̄ΠΛΑΟϹ ϤΝΑϢΝΤΟΥ
ΑΠΩϩε Ν̄εϹΑΥ ϹετεΟΥε ΝεϤ
εΜΝΚΡΑϤ Μ̄ΜΟΥ ϩΟΟΠ Ν̄ϩΗΤΟΥ

10 ΜΝ̄Ν̄Ϲε Νεï ϤΝ̄ΝΗΥ ΑϩΡΗï 6ε
ϩΗΛεΙΑϹ ΜΝ̄ εΝΩΧ ϹεΚΟΥ Λ

25 reach out over the earth
seventy two cubits. It
will consume the sinners
and the devils
like straw.

30 A just judgement will take place
at that time.
The mountains of the earth will make
their voices heard. At (that) time

Ach 41,1 . . . .
. . . .
The roads? (see Rosenstiehl) will say to
each other, "Did you hear today

5 the sound of a man who makes
his way to the judgement of the son of God?
The sins of each will oppose
him in the place where they were committed,
whether by day or by night

10 . . . the just and the [. . .]
will see the sinners in their punishment,
as well as those who persecuted them,
and those who delivered them to
death. Then the sinners . . .

15 . . . will see the abode of the righteous
and the manner in which grace will ensue.
At that time, that which the righteous

42,1 will often request
will be given to them. At that time
the Lord will judge heaven
and earth. He will judge those

5 who have transgressed in heaven and those
who have done so on earth. He will judge
the shepherds of the people. He will ask them
concerning the flock, and they will hand them over to him
without deadly guile.

10 After that Elijah and
Enoch descend. They lay aside

ⲉⲣⲏⲓ̈ ⲛ̄ⲧⲥⲁⲣⲝ ⲙ̄ⲡⲓⲕⲟⲥⲙⲟⲥ ⲥⲉ

ⲭⲓ ⲛ̄ⲛⲟⲩⲥⲁⲣⲝ ⲙ̄ⲡⲛ̄ⲁ̄ ⲥⲉⲡⲱⲧ

ⲥⲉⲡϣⲏⲣⲉ ⲛ̄ⲧⲁⲛⲟⲙⲓⲁ ⲥⲉⲋⲱ

15 ⲧⲃⲉ ⲙ̄ⲙⲁϥ ⲉⲙⲁϥⲋⲱϫⲉ ⲋⲙ̄

ⲫⲟⲟⲩⲉ ⲉⲧⲙ̄ⲙⲟ ϥⲛⲁⲃⲱⲗ ⲁ

ⲃⲁⲗ ⲙ̄ⲡⲟⲩⲙ̄ⲧⲟ ⲁⲃⲁⲗ ⲛ̄ⲧⲋⲉ ⲛ̄[ⲟⲩ]

43,1 ⲕⲣⲩⲥⲧⲁⲗⲗⲟⲥ ⲉⲁϥⲃⲱⲗ ⲁⲃⲁⲗ ϋⲓⲧⲛ̄

ⲟⲩⲕⲱⲋⲧ ϥⲛⲁⲧⲉⲕⲟ ⲛ̄ⲧⲋⲉ ⲛ̄ⲟⲩ

ⲁⲣⲁⲕⲱⲛ ⲉⲙ̄ⲛⲛⲓϥⲉ ⲛ̄ϋⲏⲧϥ ⲥⲉⲛⲁ

ϫⲟⲟⳞ ⲛⲉϥ ϫⲉ ⲁⲡⲕⲟⲩⲁ̈ⲓ̈ϣ ⲓ̈ⲛⲉ ⲁ

5 ⲣⲁⲕ ϯⲛⲟⲩ ϭⲉ ⲁⲕⲛⲁⲧⲉⲕⲟ ⲙ̄ⲛ ⲛⲉ

ⲧⲣ̄ ⲡⲓⲥⲧⲉⲩⲉ ⲁⲣⲁⲕ ⲥⲉⲛⲁⲧⲉⲕⲟⲩ

ⲁⲧϣⲱⲧⲉ ⲙ̄ⲡⲛⲟⲩⲛ ⲥⲉⲋⲱϫⲉ ⲙ̄

ⲙⲁⳞ ⲁⲣⲟⲟⲩ ϋⲙ ⲫⲟⲟⲩⲉ ⲉⲧⲙ̄ⲙⲟ

ϥⲛ̄ⲛⲏⲩ ⲁⲃⲁⲗ ⲛ̄ⲧⲡⲉ ϭⲉ ⲡⲭ̄ⲥ̄

10 ⲡⲣ̄ⲣⲟ ⲙ̄ⲛ̄ ⲛⲉⲧⲟⲩⲁⲁⲃⲉ ⲧⲏⲣⲟⲩ

ϥⲣⲱⲕ ⲋ ⲙ̄ⲡⲓⲕⲁ ⳝ ϥⲣ̄ ϋⲟ ⲛ̄ⲣⲁⲙⲡⲉ

ϋⲓϫⲱϥ ϫⲉ ⲁⲛⲣⲉϥⲣ̄ ⲛⲁⲃⲉ ⲉⲙⲁϋⲧⲉ

ϋⲓϫⲱϥ ϥⲛⲁⲧⲁⲛⲟ ⲛ̄ⲟⲩⲡⲉ ⲛ̄ⲃⲣ̄ⲣⲉ

ⲙ̄ⲛ̄ ⲟⲩⲕⲁ ⳝ ⲛ̄ⲃⲣ̄ⲣⲉ ⲙ̄ⲛ̄ ⲁⲓⲁⲃⲟⲗⲟⲥ

15 ..ϥⲩ ϋⲟⲟⲡ ⲛ̄ϋⲏⲧⲟⲩ ϥⲛⲁⲣⲣⲟ

ⲙ]ⲛ̣ ⲛⲉⲧⲟⲩⲁⲁⲃⲉ ⲉϥⲛⲁ ⲁϋⲣⲏⲓ̈

.ⲛ̄ⲛⲏⲩ ⲁϋⲣⲏⲓ̈ ⲉⲩϋⲟⲟⲡ ⲙ̄ⲛ̄ ⲛ̄

44,1 ⲁⲅⲅⲉⲗⲟⲥ ⲛ̄ⲟⲩⲁ̈ⲓ̈ϣ ⲛⲓⲙ ⲉⲩϋⲟⲟⲡ ⲙ̄ⲛ̄

ⲡⲭ̄ⲥ̄ ⲛϋⲟ ⲛ̄ⲣⲁⲙⲡⲉ

ϯⲁⲡⲟⲕⲁⲗⲩⲯⲓⳞ

ⲛϋⲏⲗⲉⲓⲁⳞ

the flesh of the world and
put on the flesh of the spirit. They pursue
the lawless one and kill
15 him without his being able to utter a sound. At
that time he will melt
before them like
43,1 ice which melts through
fire. He will perish like a
dragon which is without breath. He will
be told, "Your time is up.
5 Now you will perish with those
who believed in you." They will
be thrown into the deep pit, and it will
be shut over them. At that time
the Christ comes from heaven,
10 the king together with all the saints.
He burns the earth and spends a thousand years
on it, because the sinners held sway
over it. He will create a new heaven
and a new earth. No devil
15 or death (see Rosenstiehl) exists in them. With the
saints he will rule, descending and
ascending. They will be with the
44,1 angels always. They will be with
the Christ a thousand years.

The Apocalypse
of Elijah

FACSIMILES

of

P. CHESTER BEATTY 2018

Facsimiles reduced to 65% of original size.

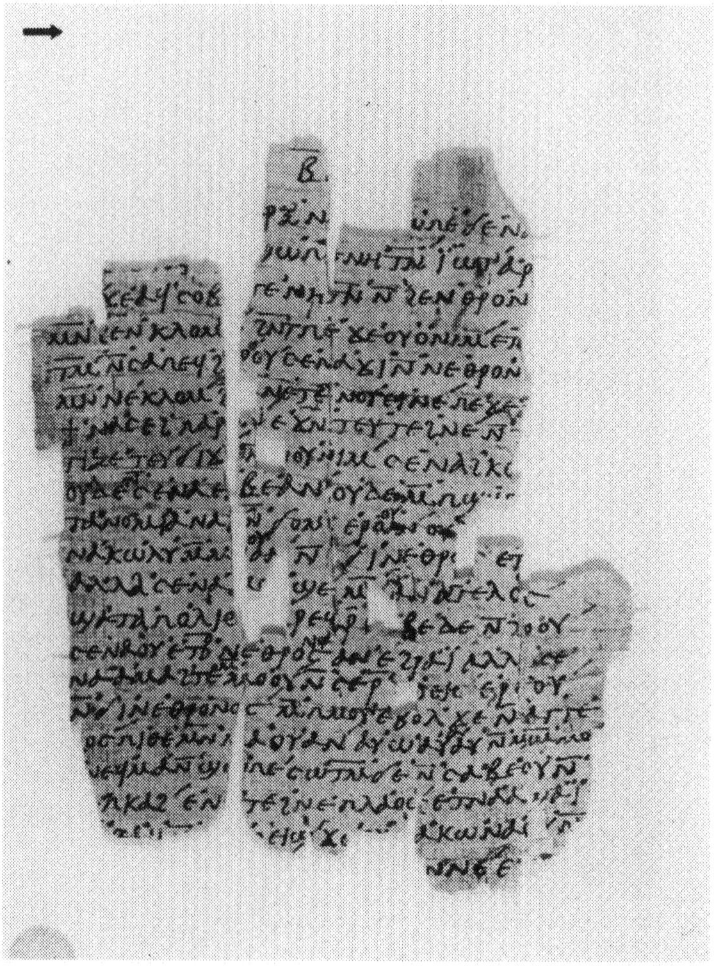

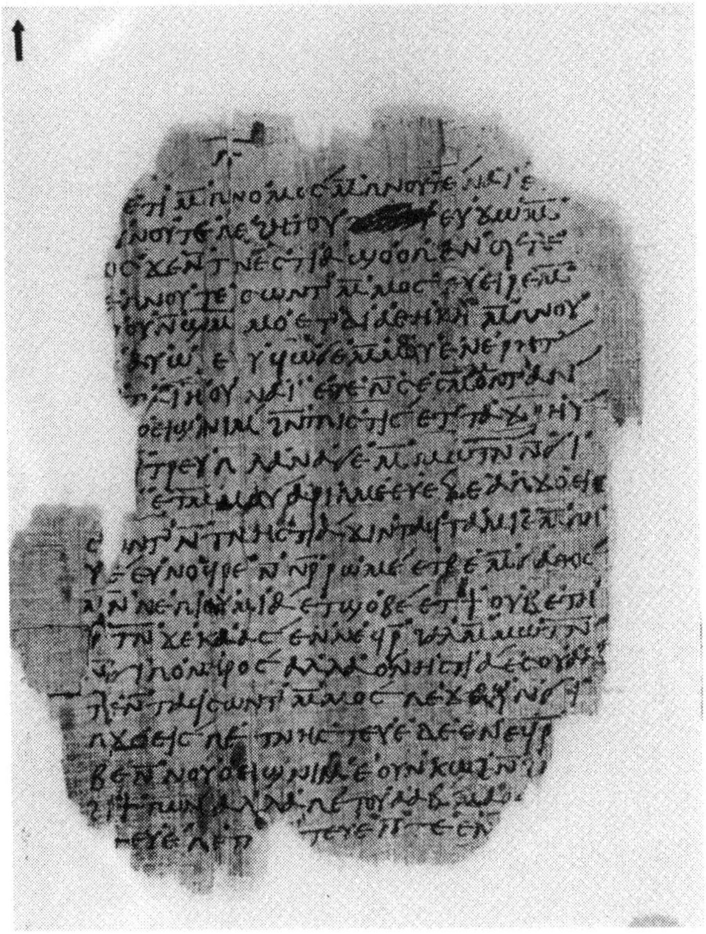

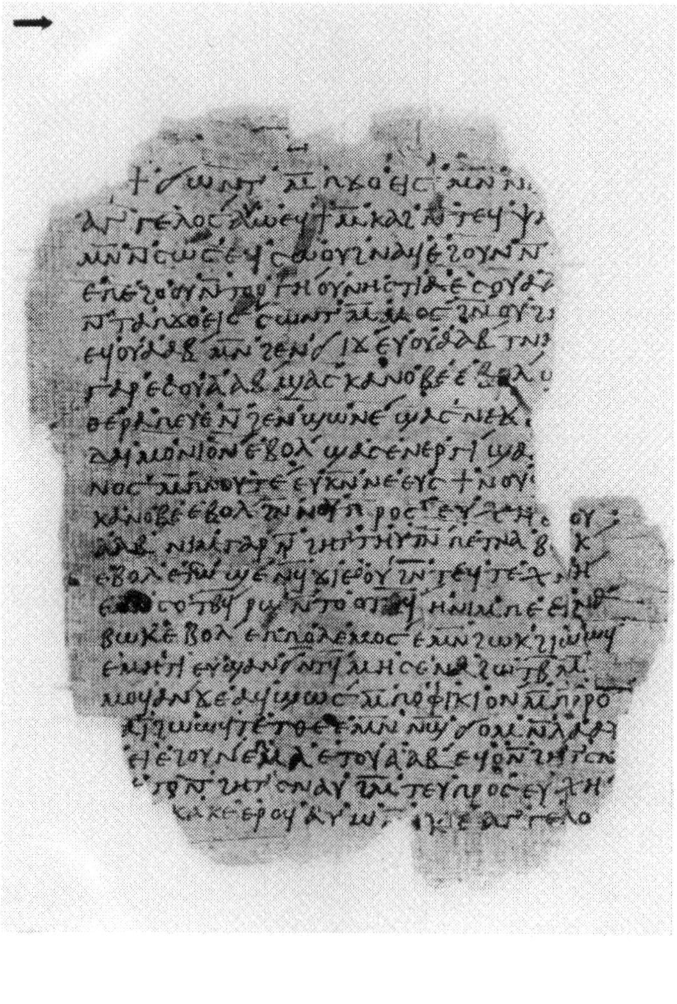

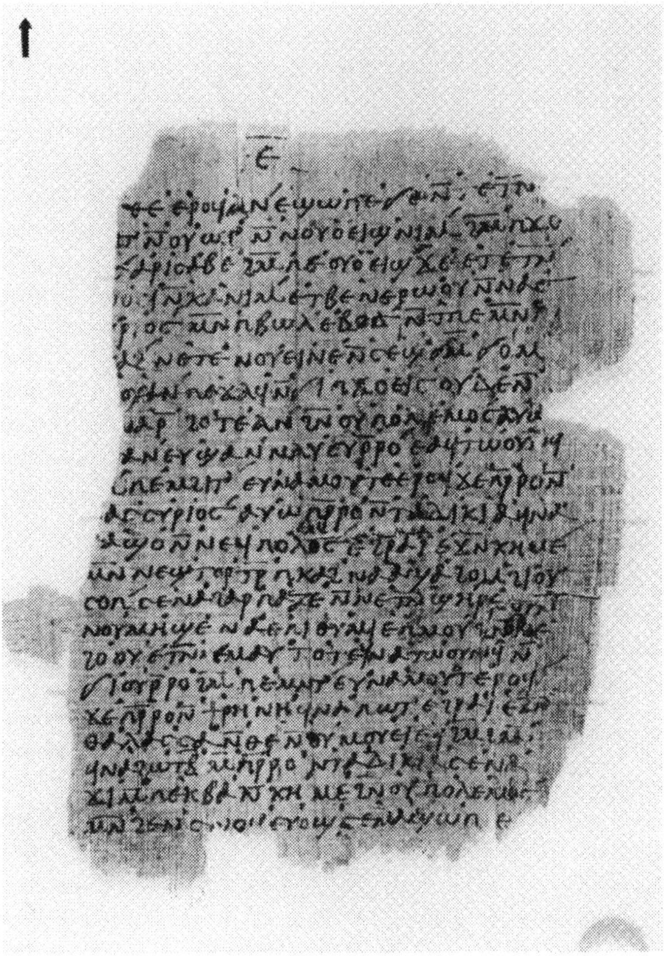

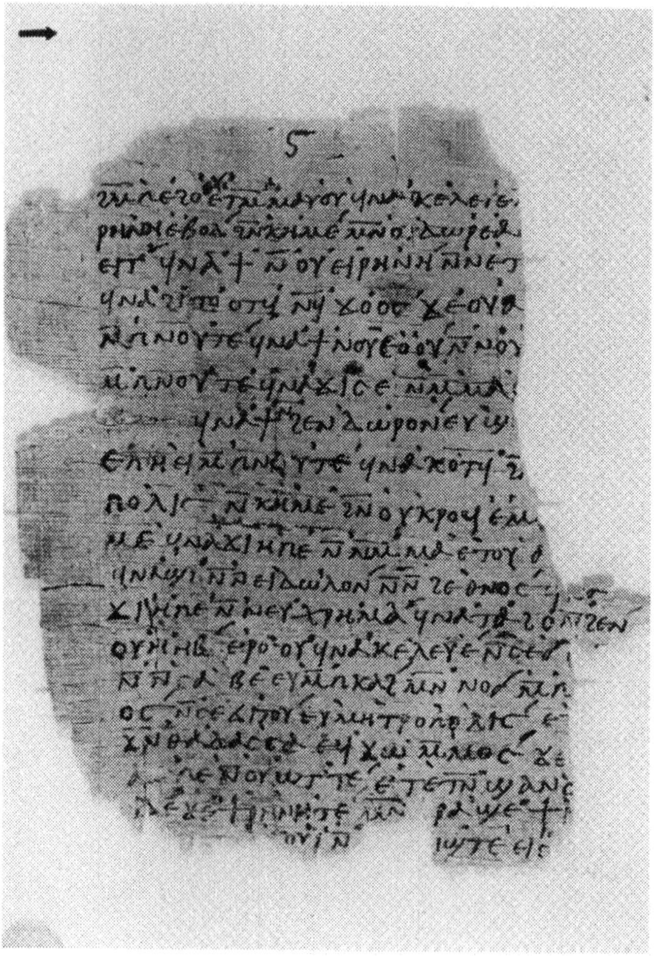

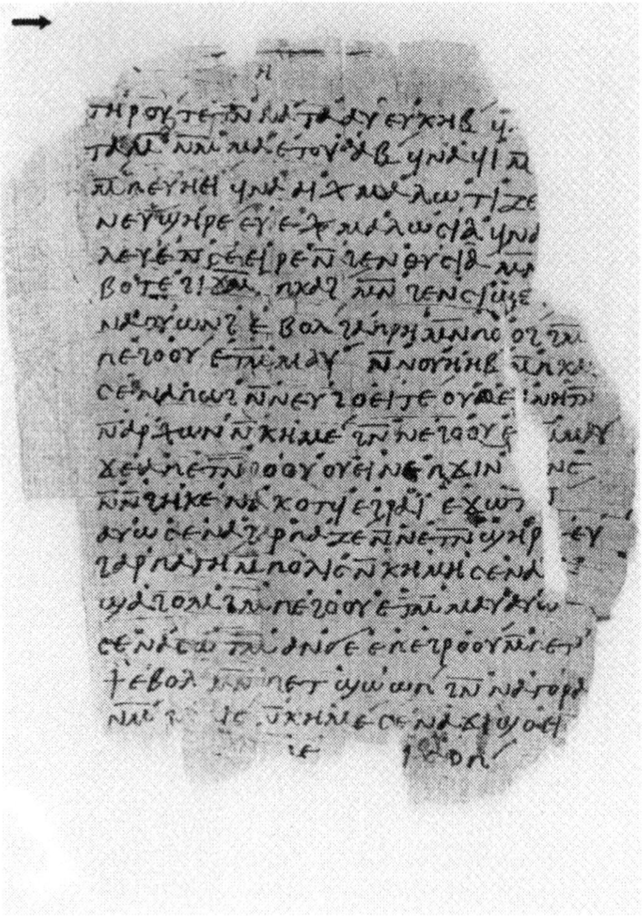

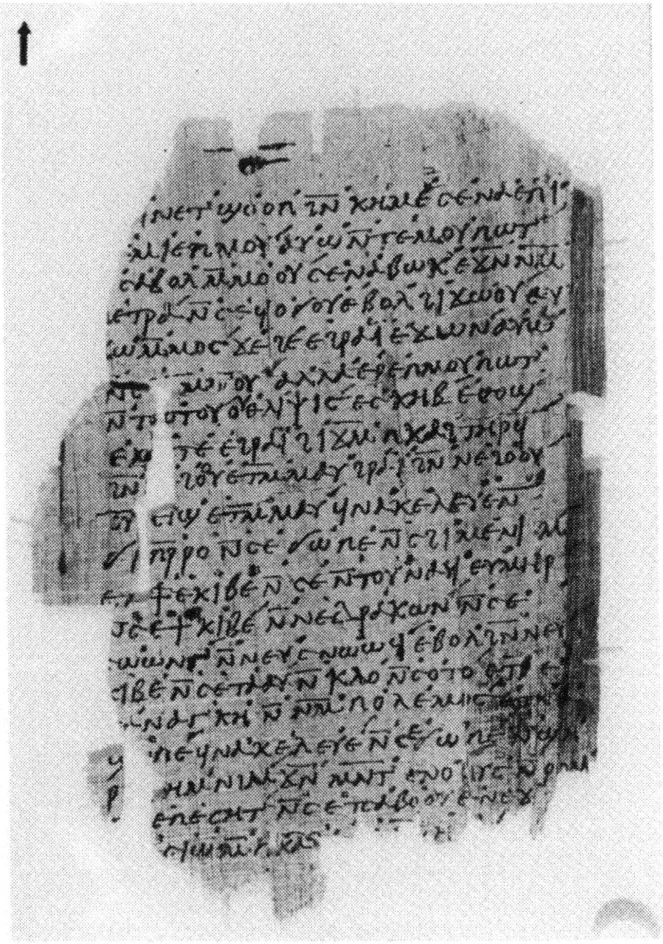

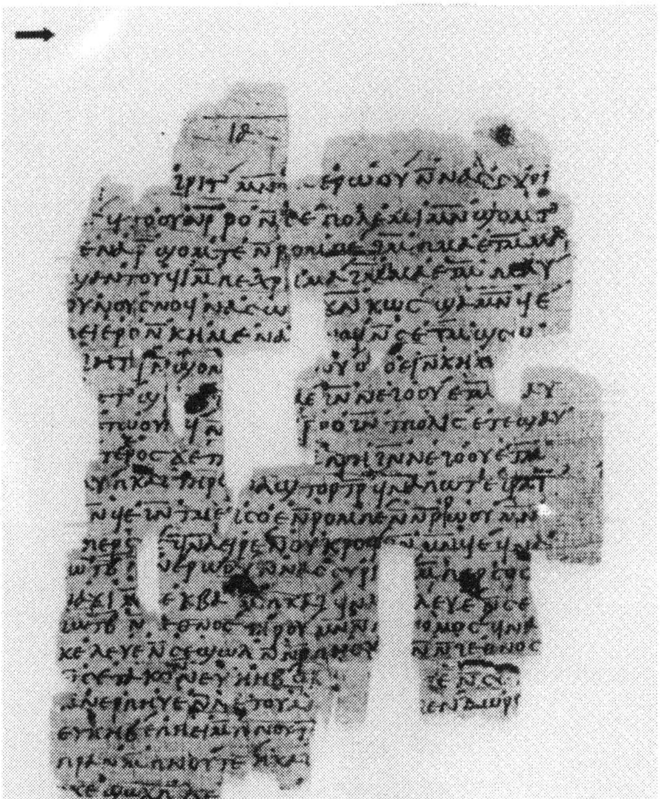

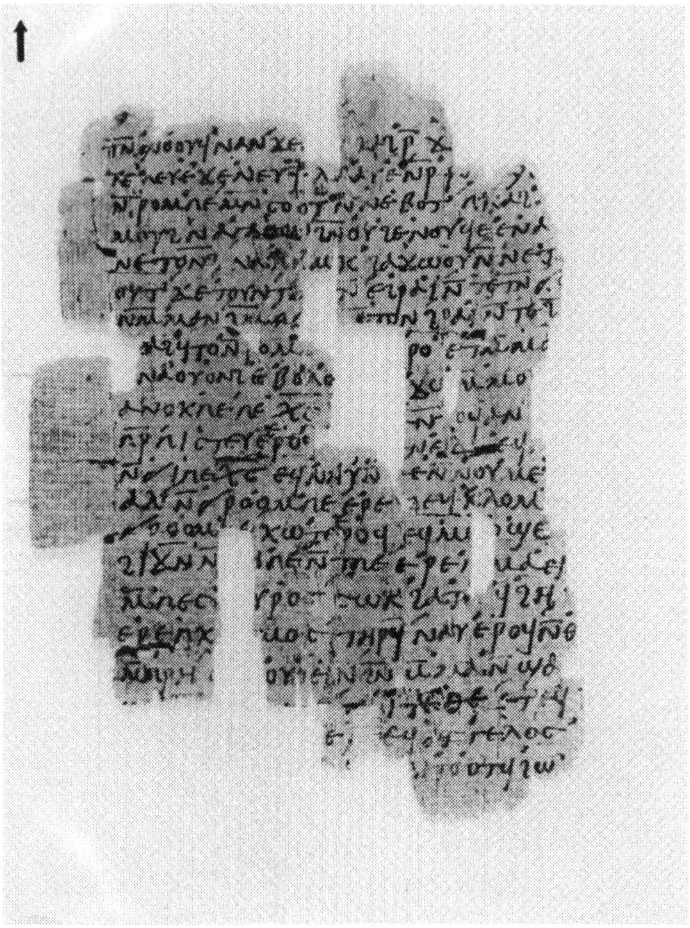

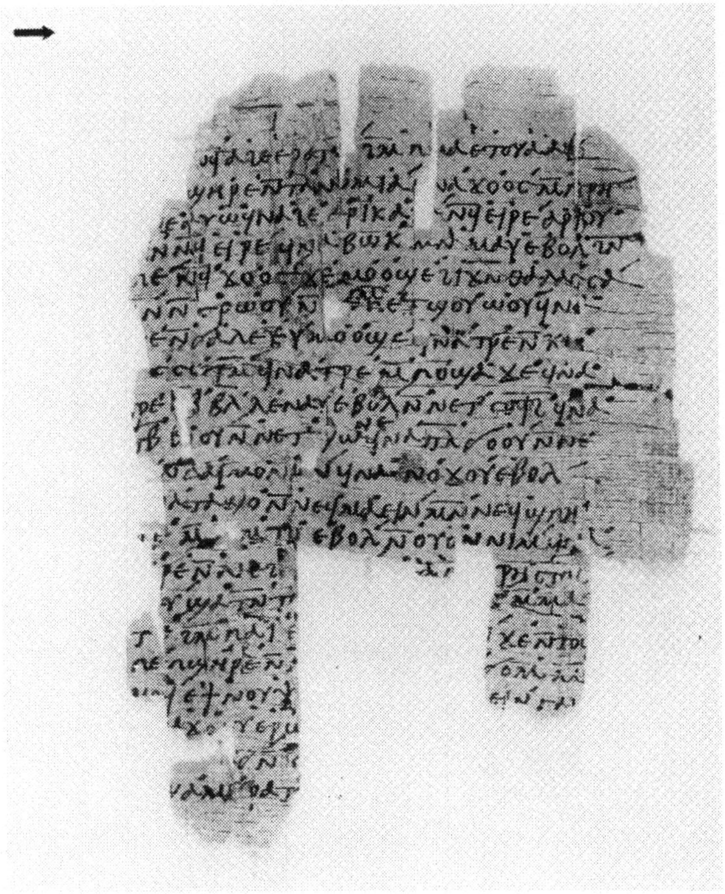

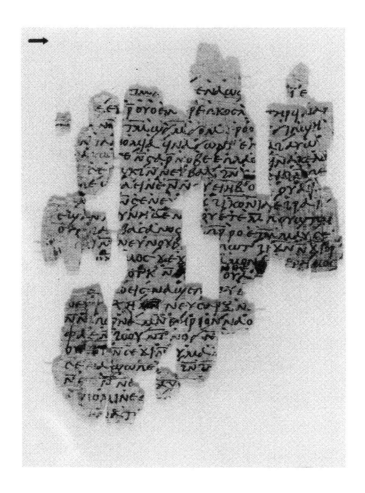

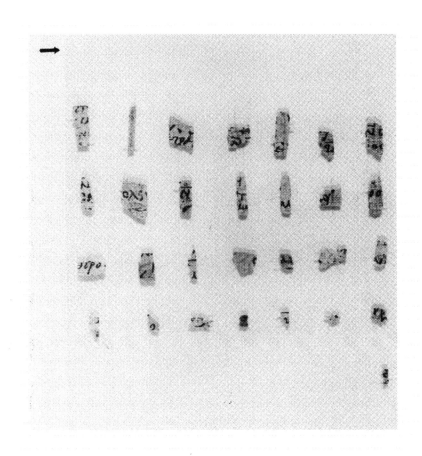

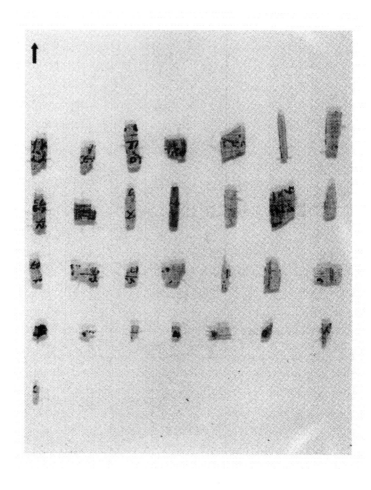

Appendix: The Greek *Apocalypse of Elijah*

In 1912 E. Pistelli published in *Papiri Greci e Latini*[1] a 6.5 x
6.5 cm scrap of papyrus, written in Greek, which contained a total of
twelve incomplete lines of the *Apocalypse of Elijah*. The significance
of the fragment lay neither in its extent nor even in its contents
but rather in the fact that it furnished proof positive for a Greek
original of the *Apocalypse* - something which could of necessity be no
more than a (well-founded) scholarly theory prior to the discovery of
PSI 7.

The credit for identifying the fragment is given by its editor to
Theodor Zahn. The verso side clearly has to do with one of the arrivals
of Elijah and Enoch, though Pistelli mistakenly indicated the latter
name as having been partially preserved.[2] More particularly, it relates
their second appearance on the field of battle, for the purpose of anni-
hilating the "lawless one."[3] Although the fragment shows clearly that
in some ways the extant Greek and Coptic texts are related, J.-M.
Rosenstiehl in the most recent translation of and commentary on the
Apocalypse of Elijah appears to overstate the case for the relationship
when he writes, "Ce fragment montre que les textes grec et copte devaient
être très proches l'un de l'autre."[4] There is, after all, the recto
side to take into account, not to mention the minor deviations from Ach
on the verso side. Pistelli was not able to place the recto side of the
fragment, and thus far I have been likewise unsuccessful.[5] Unfortunately Sa[3] ends too soon to be of any help.

---

[1] See above p. 1.

[2] That a piece of papyrus has broken off and been lost since Pistelli
read it is not confirmed by his transcription of the recto side.

[3] See above p. 65, Ach 42.

[4] *L'Apocalypse d'Elie* (Textes et Etudes pour servir a l'histoire du
Judaïsme intertestamentaire vol. 1). Paris, 1972, p. 21.

[5] It is hoped that the facsimiles here published for the first time
will aid interested scholars in solving this central problem of the
fragment. I am grateful to the Istituto Papirologico "G. Vitelli"
(Florence) for the photographs sent upon request and to the Biblioteca Medicea Laurenziana for permission to reproduce them here. The
editio princeps is faulty in many particulars.

Text:

→ (recto)	↑ (verso)
top of page	top of page

```
        ]ΛΩΣΣΩΝ                    ΠΟΙΜΕΝΑΣΤΟΥ.[
        ]ΜΑΤΑΜΕΡΙ                  ΤΗΝΝΟΜΗΝΤ[
        ].Α˙ΕΚΕΙΜΕΝ               ΑΝΕΥΔΟΛΟΥ˙Μ[
          ].Σ˙ΔΙΑΤ.Ν               ΟΤΕΗΛΕΙΑΣ.[
   5    ]...                  5   ΤΟΥΚΟΣΜ[ ].[
          ].ΣΤΑ                    .ΑΤΑ...[
```

([κρινεῖ τοὺς])

```
]λωσσων           ποιμένας τοῦ λ[αοῦ. ἐπερωτήσει αὐτοὺς διὰ
]ματα μερι        τὴν νομὴν τ[ῶν προβάτων καὶ παραδοθήσονται
].α˙ εκει μεν     ἄνευ δόλου· μ[ετὰ δὲ ταῦτα καταβήσονται
].ϛ˙ δια τον      ὅ τε ἡλεύας κ[αὶ ἐνώχ. ἀποθήσονται τὴν σάρκα
5  ]αυ.         5 τοῦ κόσμ[ο]υ [καὶ περιβαλοῦνται τὴν σάρκα π̄ν̄ς̄
]ροτα             καταδιώ[ξουσιν τὸν υἱὸν τῆς ἀνομίας
```

One should perhaps assume that recto preceded verso since the identifiable portion belongs to the concluding pages of the *Apocalypse of Elijah* and hence plausibly stood in the second half of the quire. If line length was indeed approximately 32-36 letters, as the above reconstruction indicates, and if recto preceded verso, what we have on the recto side of PSI 7 may have stood where Ach now has a lacuna, i.e., between 40 and 41. But in that case Gk must have differed at that point from Sa[1]!

In conclusion, the papyrus was photographed through glass and as a result small holes cannot with absolute certainty be distinguished from punctuation. For some reason Pistelli chose to ignore not only the rough breathing on ἡλειας but also the high stops on 4→ and 3↑ where their presence is confirmed by spacing. εκειμεν on 3→ is likewise apparently preceded by a high stop. On 5→ Pistelli comments, "Dopo una traccia di lettera la linea è bianca, il che dimostra che qui era il titolo d'un capitolo, oppure che la linea finiva prima per tornare a capo" (Note 5, p. 17). Such a conclusion is, of course, unwarranted since both preceding lines appear to be especially long and, more importantly, we do not possess enough of the document to determine scribal practice.

A. Pietersma

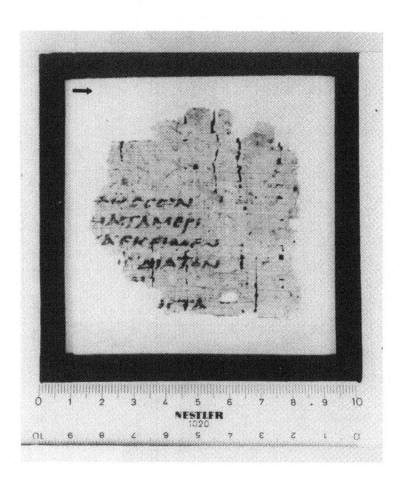

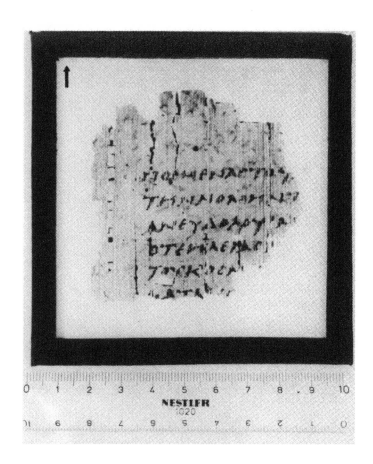

References are to ms(s) pagination. * = fully restored reading.

ἔθνος	6,11; 11,16.17
εἴδωλον	6,11
εἰμήτι	4,16
εἰρήνη	5,18; 6,1.3.18; 19,20*
εἴτε	Ach 41,9(bis)
ἐνεργεῖν	4,9
ἐπιθυμεῖν	1,13; 5,15; 9,1
ἐπιθυμία	3,13
ἔρημος	17,12; Sa¹13,32
ἔτι	2,11
ἤ	4,14; 20,14
θάλασσα	5,19; 6,16; 13,5; 20,1*.18
θεραπεύειν	4,8
θηρίον	17,16; 19,23*
θλῖψις	9,7; 20,12
θρόνος	2,3.5.11(ϑρoc).14.16; 4,9; 15,15; 18,2
θυσία	8,5
καρπός	1,15; Sa¹14,1
κελεύειν	6,1.13; 7,14; 8,4; 9,10.17; 11,15.17.18; 12,2; 17,5.8; 18,13; Sa¹14,21
κόλασις	Ach 41,11
κονία	17,8
κόσμος	1,6.7.8.20; 12,17; 17.2; Ach 42,12
κρίνειν	Ach 42,3.4.6
κρίσις	17,17; Ach 41,6
κρύσταλλος	Ach 43,1
κωλύειν	2,11
κωφός	13,7
λαός	1,3; 6,14; 15,1.7; 16,5.9; 17,5; Ach 42,7
μέν	14,4
μή	4,16; 18,18*
μητρόπολις	6,15
νηστεία	3,3(ⲛⲉⲥⲧⲓⲁ) .11.15; 4,4.6
νηστεύειν	3,17.19.20
νοεῖν	5,4

νόμος	3,1
ὀργή	4,3*.4; 20.16
ὅταν	5,9
οὐδέ	1,7.14.22; 2,9(bis).10; 5,7; 15,4; 19,16(bis)
οὔτε	3,3
ὀφφίκιον	4,17
πάθος	3,12
παραβαίνειν	Ach 42,5
παραδιδόναι	Ach 41,13
παρακαλεῖν	20,15
παρθένος	10,4; 14,9.17
πείθειν	18,20
πείθεσθαι	2,17; 5,1
πέρνα	17,16
πέτρα	9,4
πιστεύειν	12,11; Ach 43,6
πίστις	3,8
πλανᾶν	3,9; 16,9
πλάνος	2,19(πλλοc)
πληγή	11,22*
πνεῦμα (π̄ν̄λ̄)	17,14; Ach 42,13
πολεμεῖν	11,2; 15,11.21; 16,2.20; Sa¹14,14.16
πόλεμος	4,15; 5,8.12.21; 9,16; Sa¹14,17
πόλις	2,13; 6,9; 8,14.18; 11,9.10; 16,1*.21*
πονηρός	3,15
προσευχή	4,11.20
προφήτης	18,8
σάρξ	2,1; 16,14; 17,15; Ach 42,12.13
σταυρός	12,16
στῦλος	19,11
σφραγίζειν	2,7
σφραγίς	19,7
σῶμα	15,4; 16,15
τεχνή	4,13
τότε	5,16; 10,13; 14,17*; 15,8; 19,10*; 20,20; Sa¹14,11; Ach 41,14

ὑπομένειν	17,20*.21
φορεῖν	19,14
φυλή	15,18
χρῆμα	6,12; 11,4
ψυχή	4,2; 13,18; 15,4; 17,15
ὦ	14,15(bis).16; 16,8

INDEX OF COPTIC WORDS

References are to ms(s) pagination. * = fully restored reading.
† = qualitative.

ⲀⲘⲀϨⲦⲈ	seize, lay hold on, prevail 2,15; ⲈⲘⲀϨⲦⲈ Sa[1] 14,24; Ach 43,12
ⲀⲚ	negative particle 2,8.9.10.11.14.17.21; 3,3.7; 4,17; 5,1.7.8; 8,16; 10,16; 12,10; 15,12.19; 16,8.11; 17,19; 18,17.20; 19,16(bis).17; 20,20; Sa[1] 13,25
ⲀⲚⲞⲔ	pers. pron. I, 12,10; 15,5; 20,5
ⲀⲡⲈ	f. head 14,7
ⲀⲤⲡⲈ	f. language, speech 6,7
ⲀⲨⲱ	and 1,3.18; 2,17; 3,6; 4,2.21; 5,8.11; 7,4; 8,13. 15; 9,2.5; 10,1; 13,3; 15,13; 16,3; 17,4; 18,15*; 19,5.20; Sa[1] 14,24; Ach 41,16 (ⲀⲞⲨ)
ⲀϢⲀⲒ	multiply 2,19; ⲞϢⲦ 5,22; 9,7; Sa[1] 14,18
ⲀϨⲞⲘ	m. groan 5,13; 8,15; 20.2*
ⲀϬⲢⲎⲚⲎ	f. barren female 10,4
ⲂⲰⲔ	go 4,12.15; 9,3; 12,5; 13,4; 20,17
ⲂⲀⲖ	m. eye 17,6
ⲂⲰⲖ	loosen, with ⲈⲂⲞⲖ Ach 42,16; 43,1; subst. with ⲈⲂⲞⲖ 1,9; 5,5; 18,1
ⲂⲀⲖⲈ	m. blind person 13,9
ⲂⲰⲰⲚ	bad 20,12
ⲂⲞⲨⲢ	f. left hand 7,4
ⲂⲢⲢⲈ	new, young Ach 43,13.14
ⲂⲞⲦⲈ	f. abomination 8,6
ⲂⲞⲨϨⲈ	m. eyelid 14,1
Ⲉ-, ⲈⲢⲞ⸗	prep. *passim*
ⲈⲂⲞⲖ	adverb 1,9; 4,7.9.11.13.15; 5,5; 7,14; 8,7.17; 9,4; 10,17; 12,9; 13,9.11.13; 14,4.11; 15,9; 18,1.17*; 20,8*; Sa[1] 13,31; 14,12.23; ⲀⲂⲀⲖ Ach 42,16.17; 43,1.9
ⲈⲂⲞⲦ	m. month 12,3; Sa[1] 13,27
ⲈⲔⲒⲂⲈ	f. breast 9,12.13.15
ⲈⲘⲚⲦ	m. west 5,17
ⲈⲢⲎⲦ	m. promise 3,6
ⲈⲢⲎⲨ	each other 11,1; Ach 41,4
ⲈⲤⲎⲦ	m. ground; ⲈⲚⲈⲤⲎⲦ down 9,19; 15,10; Sa[1] 14,16

ⲉⲥⲟⲟⲩ	m. sheep Ach 42,8
ⲉⲧⲃⲉ	prep. 1,3.18; 2,19 (ⲉⲛ[.]˙ⲧⲉⲍ?); 3,12; 5,4; 9,15; 10,2; ⲉⲧⲃⲏⲧ⸗ Saˡ 13,35; 14,2.4
ⲉⲟⲟⲩ	m. honour 1,19; 4,13; 6,5; 18,2; 19,5
ⲉϣⲱⲡⲉ	if 5,1; Saˡ 14,8*
ⲉⲍⲟⲩⲛ	See ⲍⲟⲩⲛ
ⲉⲍⲣⲁⲓ	See ⲍⲣⲁⲓ
ⲉⲭⲛ-	See ⲭⲱ⸗
ⲏⲓ	m. house 6,8; 8,3; 11,20
ⲏⲡⲉ	f. number 6,10.12
ⲉⲓ	come 4,19; 10,16; 12,11; Saˡ 14,16; Ach 41,6
ⲉⲓⲁ	eye; ⲉⲓⲁⲧ⸗ 10,1 *
ⲉⲓⲏⲃ	m. fingernail 17,7
ⲉⲓⲃⲉ	become thirsty 2,9; 19,16
ⲉⲓⲙⲉ	know 6,9
ⲉⲓⲛⲉ	bring 17,7; ⲛⲧ⸗ 9,12; ⲁⲛⲓ⸗ Saˡ 13,34
ⲉⲓⲟⲟⲣ	m. canal 20,19* (ⲉⲓⲣⲱⲟⲩ)
ⲉⲓⲉⲣⲟ	m. river 11,6; ⲉⲣⲱⲟⲩ 13,6
ⲉⲓⲣⲉ	do 3,4; 8,5; 11,13; 13,3.4.14; 15,14; Ach 42,6; ⲣ – *passim;* ⲁⲁ⸗ 2,17; 13,15; 18,8(bis); 20,4.9; Saˡ 14,7; Ach 41,8(ⲉ-); ⲟⲧ 4,19.20.21*; 5,1; 13.11*; 15,12; 16,18*; 20,16; ⲁⲣⲓ 1,9; 2,2; 3,10; 5,3; 13,3(bis); ⲣⲉϥⲣ- 2,13; 20,2; Saˡ 14,6.27; Ach 41,11.14; 43.12
ⲉⲓⲥ	behold 6,19; 7,1; 13,18*; ⲉⲓⲥ ⲍⲏⲏⲧⲉ 20,11
ⲉⲓⲱⲧ	m. father 2,2; 7,18
ⲉⲓⲱⲧⲉ	f. dew Saˡ 14,4
ⲕⲉ	also, even 4,1*.21; 10,12; 11,22; 15,6
ⲕⲟⲩⲓ	small 13,20*; 19,8*
ⲕⲱ	place, allow 2,20; 16,14; Ach 42,11; ⲕⲁ- 1,14.15; 4,7.11
ⲕⲱⲃ	be double; ⲕⲏⲃⲧ 8,1; 9,7; 11,20
ⲕⲃⲁ	m. vengeance 5,21; 11,15
ⲕⲁⲕⲉ	m. darkness 4,21; 13,3; 15,18; 19,19*
ⲕⲁⲟ	m. poison (?); ⲛⲥⲟⲧⲟ 9,15
ⲕⲗⲟⲙ	m. crown 2,4.6; 12,13; 18.2
ⲕⲓⲙ	move 19,4

ⲕⲛⲛⲉ   m. fatness, sweetness 4,10

ⲕⲏⲡⲉ   f. vault 12,15

ⲕⲣⲱⲙ   m. fire 1,16

ⲕⲣⲟϥ   m. deception 6,9; 11,13; Ach 42,9

ⲕⲱⲧ   build 7,9; 11,18

ⲕⲱⲧⲉ   turn, go around 12,14.21*; 16,21*; ⲕⲱⲧⲉ ⲛⲥⲁ- try 17,5; 18,20*; ⲕⲱⲧⲉ ⲉ₂ⲣⲁⲓ return (?) 9,8; ⲕⲟⲧ⁴ turn self 6,8; 8,12

ⲕⲁ₂   m. earth 1,14*.15; 2,19; 5,6.13; 6,14; 7,12.15.16; 8,6.8; 9,8.20; 10,3.7.15; 11,11.15.21; 12,1.3; 15,14; 17,4; 18,1*; 19,5*.12.18*.20*.24*; 20,3; Sa¹ 14,1(bis).3.5.22.25.32; Ach 42,4.6; 43,11.14

ⲕⲱ₂   m. envy 3,18

ⲕⲱ₂ⲧ   m. fire Sa¹ 14,12.23(ϭⲱ₂ⲧ) .24; Ach 43,2

ⲗⲟⲩⲁⲁⲓ   m. shout 17,1

ⲗⲁⲁⲩⲉ   anyone, any 4,18; 12,2

ⲙⲁ   m. place 2,18; 4,19; 6,6.10; 8,2; 10,19*; 11,3.4; 12,18.19*; 13,1; 14,11.19*; 15,10; 17,18; 20,17*; Ach 41,8.15

ⲙⲉ   love; ⲙⲉⲣⲉ- 1,6

ⲙⲉ   f. truth Sa¹ 14,30(ⲙⲏⲉ); ⲣⲙⲙⲙⲉ 18,19; ⲛⲁⲙⲉ truly 18,9

ⲙⲟⲩ   die 9,6; 11,22*; 19,23*; 20,11; ⲙⲟⲟⲩⲧ† be dead 12,5; 16,4; 19.24; ⲙⲟⲩ subst. death 2,16; 5,15; 9,2(bis).6; Ach 41,14; 42,9; ⲣⲉϥⲙⲟⲟⲩⲧ dead person 13,15; 18,9

ⲙⲟⲩⲉⲓ   m. lion 5,19

ⲙⲁⲃⲉ   numeral: thirty 7,8

ⲙⲕⲁ₂   m. pain 4,2

ⲙⲙⲛ   not to be 4,18; 20,6; ⲙⲛ 4,14.15; 10,6; 13,17*; 15,4; 16,15*; 18,10; Ach 42.9; 43,3.14

ⲙⲙⲛ ⲙⲙⲟ⁴   own self 7,12

ⲙⲛ   conj. 1,9; 2,4.6; 3,13; 4,1.6; 5,5(bis).13.22; 6,2.18; 7,18; 8,5.6.7.17; 10,4; 11,8*.16; 13,6.12; 15,8.15; 17,14*.15.16; 18,1.2.21; 19,4.10.23*; 20,12; Sa¹ 14,22.28; Ach 41,10.12. 13; 42,4.5.11; 43,14

ⲙⲛ   prep. 2,12; 6,14; 7,16; 11,1.2; 12,3; 18,7; 19,3*; Ach 41,3; 43,5.10.17; 44,1 ⲙⲛⲙⲁ⁴ 2,17; 12,7; 13,4; 15,11; 16,1.2.20 (ⲛⲙⲙⲁⲩ); Sa¹ 13,30 (ⲛⲙⲙⲏ⁴); 14,14 (ⲛⲙⲁ⁴) .17(ⲛⲙⲁ⁴)

ⲙⲁⲉⲓⲛ   m. sign, mark 7,1; 12,5; 13,12.18; 14,6(bis);

	18,21*; 20,8
ⲘⲚⲚⲤⲀ	prep. Ach 42,10; ⲘⲚⲚⲤⲱ⸗ 4,3
ⲘⲠⲟ	dumb person 13,8
ⲘⲟⲨⲢ	bind 18,13; ⲘⲎⲢ† 9,12
ⲘⲓⲤⲉ	bear 10,1
ⲘⲉⲤⲓⲱ	f. midwife 9,20
ⲘⲎⲦ	m. ten; ⲘⲚⲦ- 9,18; 20,18
ⲘⲀⲦⲉ	only; ⲘⲘⲀⲦⲉ 13,15
ⲘⲟⲨⲦⲉ	call 5,10.17; 11,10
ⲘⲦⲟ	m. face, presence 13,13; 14,3; 20,8; Ach 42,17
ⲘⲦⲟⲚ	m. rest 12,7; 17,18*
ⲘⲀⲨ	place; ⲉⲦⲘⲘⲀⲨ 3,10; 5,16(ⲉⲦⲚⲉⲘⲀⲨ); 6,1 (ⲉⲦⲘⲘⲀⲨⲟⲨ); 7,7.10.13; 8,8.10.15; 9,9.10; 10,8.18.20; 11,3.4.8.10; 12,8; 16,17; 17,1.10; 18,4.15.21; 19,18*; 20,22; Sa¹ 14,19.31; ⲉⲦⲘⲘⲟ Ach 41,17; 42,2.16; 43,8
ⲘⲟⲟⲨ	m. water 1,17; 20,18*.20*; pl. ⲘⲟⲨⲉⲓⲟⲟⲨⲉ 20,1*
ⲘⲉⲉⲨⲉ	m. thought 1,9; 2,2*; 3,10
ⲘⲎⲎϣⲉ	m. multitude 1,12; 5,15(ⲘⲎϣⲉ); 18,16*
Ⲙⲓϣⲉ	fight 18,6
Ⲙⲟⲟϣⲉ	walk, go 2,12; 12,14; 13,5.7; Ach 41,5 (ⲘⲀⲀ2ⲉ)
ⲘⲟⲨ2	fill, be filled 12,4; ordinal number with Ⲙⲉ2- 7,8; 11,12; 12,8(ⲘⲀ2-); 16,6; 19,2
ⲘⲀ2ⲉ	f. cubit 20,19; Sa¹ 14,26
Ⲙⲉ2Ⲁⲗ	bevy, flock 12,13
Ⲙ2ⲓⲦ	m. north 5,10
ⲘⲀⲀϫⲉ	m. ear 14,2 (ⲘⲚⲘⲀⲀϫⲉ)
Ⲛ-, ⲘⲘⲟ⸗	prep. *passim*
Ⲛ-, ⲚⲀ⸗	prep. *passim*
ⲚⲀ	go Ach 43,16 (ⲚⲚⲀ)
ⲚⲟⲨ	go; ⲚⲎⲨ† 1,22.24*; 7,7.9; 12,11.12.20*; 14,1; 15,10; Sa¹ 14,5; Ach 42,10; 43,9(ⲚⲚⲎⲨ).17 (ⲚⲚⲎⲨ)
ⲚⲟⲨⲃ	m. gold 17,11
Ⲛⲟⲃⲉ	m. sin 1,3.4(bis); 2,13; 3,17; 4,7.11; 17,5; 20,2; Sa¹ 14,6.28; Ach 41,7.11.14; 43,12
ⲚⲔⲀ	m. thing 1,11; 5,4
ⲚⲔⲟⲦⲔ	sleep 17,13
ⲚⲓⲘ	who? 4,12.14

N I M	every 1,11; 2,4; 3,8.18; 5,2.4; 7,17; 9,11.18; 13,13; 14,6; 15,5.13.16; 16,12.18.19; 18,8; 20,10; Ach 44,1
NOYN	pit Ach 43,7
NCλ-	prep. 2,5; 17,5; 18,19.20*; 20,16; Ach 42,14(cε); Ncω⸗ 14,18; 20,11; Sa¹ 14,10.27
NTε	prep. 2,18
NTOK	you 15,15(NTK).19.20(NTOOK); 16,9.11; 18,11; 20,5.6*
NTOOY	they 2,13; 17,9; Ach 41,10(NTλY)
NTO9	he 12,10; 13,16; 14,6.8
NλY	look, see 5,9; 12,17; 13,9; 16,5; 17,2; 18,1*; N O Ach 41,11.15
NλY	m. hour, time 14,20; 15,2
NOYTε	m. god 3,2; ΠNOYTε God 1,5.18; 2,21; 3,1.4.5; 4,10; 6,5.6.8; 7,6; 11,20.21; 15,19*; 16,9; 18,5; 20,17; Sa¹ 14,8; Ach 41,6
Nλϣε	be many; Nλϣω⸗ 12,4
N I 9 ε	m. breath Ach 43,3
NOY9 P	be good; NO9ρε f. good 3,12; NOY9ε adj. good 4,10; 12,4
NOY2M	save 20,7; Nλ2M⸗ 1,11.20.24*; 20,7
NOYⲬε	throw, place 14,21*; 15,6; Nεx- 4,8; 9,19; 17,8; NOx⸗ 13,11
NO6	great 6,14; 16,1; 17,17; 19,8; Sa¹ 14,21
N6 I	resumptive particle, *passim*
O N	again 13,1*; 14,5; 15,6; 16,7; Sa¹ 14,14
OO2	m. moon 8,7
O2ε	m. fold Ach 42,8
Π-, T-, N-	definite article, *passim*
Πλ-	pre-nominal possessive article 1,8; Nλ-2,21*; 15,13
Πε	copula 3,2; 4,14.18; 6,4*; 10,5.13; 11,20*; 12,10 (bis); 13,17.20*; 14,8.10; 18,11.17; 20,5*.14*; Tε 4,18; 6,17.18; 12,19; Nε 2,6.21
Πε	f. heaven 2,4; 5,5; 10,2; 12,15; 13,5; 15,13*.17; 17,2; 18,1; 19,2.4*.20; Sa¹ 14,22; Ach 42,3.5; 43,9.13; pl. ΠΗYε 3,11; 10,8
Πε⸗, Tε⸗, Nε⸗	pre-pronominal possessive article Πλ 1,8; 2,7; 7,18; 15,4; 20,23*; Tλ 2,13; 15,4; Nλ Sa¹ 13,24.26.27; Πεκ Ach 43,4; Tεκ 15,18; Πε9 1,9.19.21; 2,5; 7,11; 10,16; 12,13; Ach 41,6; Tε9 4,2.13; 7,8;

12,16; 14,16; neq 2,18; 5,12; 7,1; 12,20; 13,12
(bis).18*; 14,1.2.3; 14,7; 19,1; Sa¹ 14,11;
пес 14,10.12.20; пен 20,8; нен 10,7; петн
8,11; 14,3; нетн 5,14; 8,13; 10,15; пеγ 3,2;
8,3; 19,4; Sa¹ 14,33; Ach 42,17(поγ); теγ
2,7.8; 4,20; 19.6.7.11; неγ 6,12; 8,4.9;
9,14(bis); 17,6.7.11.14.15; 19,9*

пλι	demonstrative pronoun 1,18; 13,16; 14,7; 16,10; 18,10.17; тλι 4,18; 12,19; нλι 3,1.7.10 ; 16,14 ; 17,9(нн); 18,4; 19,6; Ach 42,10(неι)
пеι	demonstrative article 1,2.12(пλιеι); 12,7; 16,15
пω⸗	possessive pronoun; ноγ⸗ 2,6; 5,6; 19,1*
пеλне	meaning unknown 13,20
пенιпе	m. iron 17,6
пωрк	be plucked out 19,22*
пωрх	m. separation 10,13
пωт	run, flee 5,18; 9,2.6; 10,19; 11,11; 14,12.18; 17,11; 18,6.19; Sa¹ 13,31; 14,10; Ach 42,13; пнт† 1,16
пωϣ	divide, be separate 18,16
пωz	tear 8,9; 10,14
пλzоγ	m. hind part, back; zι пλzоγ behind Sa¹ 14,13
пехе-	said 2,6; пехλ⸗ 3,16; 5,7; 17,21*
рн	m. sun 1,14; 8,7; 11,10; 12,18; 13,2; 14,19*; 19.19; Sa¹ 14,2
рω	emphatic particle 4,14; 15,19; 16,8.11
рωкz	burn 17,6; 18,14; Ach 43,11
рιме	weep 8,19; 20,20*; Sa¹ 14,6
рωме	m. man 1,16.23; 3,12; Ach 41,5; реq- 2,13; 20,2; Sa¹ 14,6.27; Ach 41,11.14; 43,12
рмммe	honest 18,19
ромпе	f. year 7,8; 9,18; 11,3.12; 12,3.8; Sa¹ 13,26; Ach 43,11; 44,2(рλмпе)
рλн	m. name 2,7; 6,4*; 7,6; 11,21; 14,10; 19,6*
рпе	m. temple 7,10; 15,1.7; pl. рпнγе 11,17.19
рро	m. king 4,17; 5,9.10.11.17.18.20; 7,7(bis); 9,11; 10,9.19*; 11,2.9.23*; 12,2.8; 17,10; Ach 43,10. 15; pl. ерωоγ 5,4; 11,1.14; ррωоγ 11,12; мнтрро f. kingdom 17,19 *
роеιс	watch 19,15
рооγе	m. stubble 1,17; Sa¹ 14,29(рнιоγе)
рλϣе	rejoice 10,4.6; m. joy 6,18

cooʒϵ	reprove 14,13; 15,3; 16,7.12
cʒλι	write; cϵʒ- 2,7; cʜʒ† 19,6
cʒιмϵ	f. woman 9,11
cϵιм	m. grey hair 13,21 *
тλϵιо	honour; тλιʜоʏ† 3,7
†	give 1,5.15; 6,3.5.7; 11,19*; 13,18; Sa¹ 14,32; †- 4,1.2; 9,12.13;12,2; 19,5*; Sa¹ 14,1.32; тλλ* 7,18; 8,1; 9,15; 17,22; 18,14*; 19,13*; Ach 42,2(тϵϵ*).8; † ϵвол 8,17; † cвш 20,14; † тшн 3,19; † оʏвϵ 3,13
то	f. spot 13,21*; 14,2
тшвϵ	m. birth stool 10,3
твλ	m. ten thousand 19,2
твво	purify; твво* 13,10
твʜʜ	m. animal; pl. твʜооʏϵ 19,22
тшк	throw 15,19
тλко	destroy, perish 11,18; 20,16; Sa¹13,30(тλ6о) ; Ach 43,2.5(тϵко); тϵкλ* Ach 43,6; тλко m. destruction 10,17
тλλо	lift; тλλо* 19,8
тλλ6о	heal; тλ6о 13,10
тм	negative particle 1,13*.14; 17,3
тшм	shut; тλм- 8,2
тλміо	make, create 20,9; тλміϵ-1,10*; 3,11; тλміϵ* 1,6
тλмо	tell; тλмϵ- 1,21
тϵʜоʏ	now 20,11.13.15; Sa¹ 13,29.31; Ach 43,5 (†ʜоʏ)
тшн	where 20,12.14
тшн	subst.; † тшн dispute 3,19
тλʜо	make Ach 43,13
тʜʜооʏ	send 1,19; 19,1; тʜʜооʏ* 12,1
тʜʒ	m. wing 19,3.9; Sa¹ 14,11
тʜр*	whole, all 7,13.15.16; 8,1; 9,8; 11,11.16.21*; 12,17.21*; 14,17; 16,5.21*; 17,2; 19,9; Ach 43,10
тшрϵ	f. hand; ʜтоот* 4,14; 9,7; ʒιтоот* 6,4; ʒоʏ тоот* 12,21; ʒιтʜ- Ach 43,1
тcλво	teach; тcλво* 9,19
тооʏ	m. mountain; pl. тоʏϵι Sa¹ 14,32
тλоʏо	send; тϵоʏϵ- Sa¹ 14,23; Ach 42,8
тоʏϵιо	remove; †оʏϵ- 7,6

ⲧⲱⲟⲩⲛ	arise 17,9; Sa¹ 14,9; ⲧⲱⲟⲩⲛ⸗ 5,9.16; 7,11; 10,8; 11,9; 12,6 (ⲧⲟⲩⲛ⸗); 15,2; 16,6; 17,17
ⲧⲟⲩⲛⲟⲥ	wake, raise; ⲧⲟⲩⲛⲉⲥ- 13,15; 18,9
ⲧⲁϣⲟ	increase 5,12; 13,12
ⲧⲁ2ⲟ	establish 6,12
ⲧⲉ2ⲛⲉ	f. forehead 2,7; 19,6
ⲧⲁⲭⲣⲟ	strengthen; ⲧⲁⲭⲣⲏⲩ† 3,8
ⲧⲱ6ⲉ	be joined 15,19* (ⲧⲱⲕ)
ⲧⲁ6ⲥⲉ	f. footprint 20,13
ⲟⲩ	what? 20,3; ⲉⲧⲃⲉⲟⲩ why? 1,3; 10,2
ⲟⲩⲁ	one, someone 6,4; 7,3.4; 11,20*; 17,13(bis); ⲡⲟⲩⲁ ⲡⲟⲩⲁ each 17,17(ⲟⲩⲁ ⲟⲩⲁ); 19,3.4; Ach 41,7
ⲟⲩⲟⲉ ⲓ	woe! 8,9; 11,7; 20,10.23*
ⲟⲩⲁⲁⲃ†	be holy 3,15.19.20*; 4,4.6(bis).7.11.19; 6,3*.6*.10; 7,16; 8,2; 10,19*; 11,19; 13,1; 14,11.16; 15,10; 19,12; Sa¹ 13,34; 14,13; Ach 43,10.16
ⲟⲩⲏⲏⲃ	m. priest 6,5.13; 7,15; 8,8; 10,15; 11,18
ⲟⲩⲃⲉ	opposite; + ⲟⲩⲃⲉ oppose 3,13
ⲟⲩⲱⲃϣ	white 19,15
ⲟⲩⲱⲙ	eat 19,13; Sa¹ 14,27; ⲟⲩⲟⲙ⸗ 17,16
ⲟⲩⲟⲉ ⲓ ⲛ	m. light 12,18; 13,3; 17,2; 19,11; Sa¹ 14,3
ⲟⲩⲟⲛ	be; ⲟⲩⲛ 3,18; 5,14(ⲟⲩⲛⲛ); 7,6; 11,5; 13,21*; 14,2; 19,3; Sa¹ 14,9.29; Ach 41,16; ⲟⲩⲛⲧⲁ⸗ 7,2
ⲟⲩⲟⲛ	someone 12,9; ⲟⲩⲟⲛ ⲛ ⲓⲙ 2,4(ⲟⲩⲟⲛ ⲓⲙ); 13,13; 20,10
ⲟⲩⲉ ⲓ ⲛⲉ	pass by 8,11; 20,23*; Sa¹ 13,25; Ach 43,4
ⲟⲩⲛⲁⲙ	f. right hand 2,8(ⲟⲩⲛ ⲓⲙ); 7,3.4; 17,23*; 19,7
ⲟⲩⲛⲟⲩ	f. hour 18,5(ⲉⲩⲛⲟⲩ); ⲛⲧⲉⲩⲛⲟⲩ immediately 10,17; ⲧⲉⲛⲟⲩ now 20,11.13.15; Sa¹ 13,29.31
ⲟⲩⲱⲛ2	reveal; ⲟⲩⲱⲛ2 ⲉⲃⲟⲗ 8,7; 15,9; ⲟⲩⲟⲛ2⸗ 10,17; 12,9; 14,11
ⲟⲩⲱⲧ	single, alone 5,2; 6,17
ⲟⲩⲱⲧⲃ	change Sa¹ 13,27.29; -ⲉ2ⲣⲁ ⲓ surpass 2,14
ⲟⲩⲟⲉ ⲓϣ	m. time, occasion 2,20; 3,8.18; 5,2.3; 9,10; 10,1.5; 15,5.12.16*; 16,12.18.19; 20,23*; Sa¹ 13,24; Ach 43,4; 44,1
ⲟⲩⲱϣ	desire, love 1,15.17
ⲟⲩϣⲏ	f. night Ach 41,9
ⲟⲩⲱϣⲧ	worship 11,21*; 20,13
ⲟⲩⲱ2	place; ⲟⲩⲉ2- 1,4

oyxλι	m. salvation 15,1.7
ⲱⲙⲕ	swallow 1,15; ⲟⲙⲕ⸗ 1,17
ⲱⲛ2	live 16,17*; ⲟⲛ2† 12,5; 15,2.5; 16.11; ⲱⲛ2 m. life 19,14*
ⲱⲥⲕ	delay 10,16
ⲱϣ	cry; ⲱϣ- 5,13(ⲁϣ-); 8,14(ⲁϣ-); 17,1; 20,2
ⲱϭⲙ	evaporate 20,2
ⲱ2ⲉ	stand -ⲉⲣⲁⲧ⸗ 13,1(ⲁ2ⲉ); Ach 41,7; m. condition Ach 42,8
ϣ	be able 4,18; 5,6; 11,6; 14,7; 17,3.9; 18,9; Ach 42,15(ⲉ)
ϣⲁ	rise 1,14; subst. 12,18
ϣⲁ	m. nose; ϣⲁⲛⲧ⸗ 17,9
ϣⲁ	prep. 2,13; 4,9; 11,5; 12,19; 14,1*.14; 17,16*; 19,8; ϣⲁⲣ⸗ 1,1.22.24; ϣⲁⲧⲛ- 13,15; ϣⲁ2ⲣⲁⲓ 14,14.19
ϣⲓ	measure, weigh 6,11
ϣⲟ	thousand 19,3; Ach 43,11(ⲉⲟ); 44,2(ⲉⲟ)
ϣⲓⲃⲉ	change 15,17; ϣⲃⲧ⸗ 1,23; 14,3.5.7; ϣⲟⲃⲉ† 3,13
ϣⲓⲕⲉ	dig 20,18*
ϣⲱⲕ	be deep,dug; ϣⲏⲕ† 20,17*
ϣⲱⲗ	plunder 11,17
ϣⲙⲙⲟ	subst. stranger 2,17; 3,5; 15,12.16; 20,9
ϣⲏⲙ	young 9,18; 14,15
ϣⲁⲙⲁⲣⲁⲧ	thin-legged? 13,21
ϣⲟⲙⲛⲧ	m. three 10,9; 11,2(ϣⲟⲙⲧ).7; 16,4(ϣⲟⲙ) ; ϣⲙⲧ 18,3; f. ϣⲟⲙⲧⲉ 11,3; 12,2
ϣⲏⲛ	m. tree 19,14.22
ϣⲓⲛⲉ	ask; ϣⲛⲧ⸗ Ach 42,7
ϣⲱⲛⲉ	be sick 13,10; m. sickness 4,8; ϣⲛ2ⲏⲧ⸗ 1,9.18; 18,22
ϣⲛⲥ	m. linen 14,12
ϣⲛ2ⲏⲧ⸗	have compassion 1,9.18; 18,22(ϣⲛ2 2ⲧⲏ9)
ϣⲱⲡ	receive 8,17(ϣⲟⲟⲡ); ϣⲉⲡ- 16,10; 17,14
ϣⲓⲡⲉ	be ashamed 15,12.18; 16,8; subst. ⲁⲧϣⲓⲡⲉ shameless one 14,10.15*.18*; 15,3.9.21; 16,8.19; 18,7.12; 20,20*
ϣⲱⲡⲉ	become 1,1*; 2,1.2; 5,22; 9,17; 15,1.17; 17,15.19; Sa[1] 13,26; 14,18.30; Ach 41,16(ⲉⲱⲡⲉ); ϣⲟⲟⲡ† be 1,7; 3,3; 9,1; 10,6.10; 11,8; ⲉⲟⲟⲡ Ach 42,9; 43,15.17; 44,1; ⲙⲁ ⲛϣⲱⲡⲉ m. dwelling place 2,18;

ⲉϣⲱⲡⲉ if 5,1; Sa¹ 14,8*

ϣⲡⲏⲣⲉ	m. wonder 13,12; 18,21
ϣⲏⲣⲉ	m. son 1,19; 2,2; 5,14; 7,3.11; 8,4.13; 9,17; 10,3.6.7; 14,5; ϣⲏⲣⲉ ⲛⲧⲁⲛⲟⲙⲓⲁ 2,9; 13,2.17; 14,8.15; 17,3.23*; 18,11; 19,17*; 20,4.5; Ach 42,14; ϣⲏⲣⲉ ⲙⲡⲧⲁⲕⲟ 10,16; ϣⲏⲣⲉ ⲙⲡⲛⲟⲩⲧⲉ Ach 41,6
ϣⲟⲣⲡ	earliest, first 15,2
ϣⲱⲥ	m. herd, shepherd Ach 42,7(ϣⲁⲥ)
ϣⲱⲥ	despise 4,17
ϣⲱⲧⲉ	f. well, pit Ach 43,7
ϣⲧⲟⲣⲧⲣ	shake, tremble 7,13; 11,11; 19,19; m. 5,13; 19,24★
ϣⲏⲩⲉ	f. altar; pl. ϣⲏⲟⲩⲉ 18,14
ϣⲟⲟⲩⲉ	be dry 20,1; ϣⲟⲩⲱⲟⲩ† 13,6
ϣⲟⲩⲟ	flow, empty; ϣⲟⲩⲉⲓⲧ† 6,2.7; 20.8
ϣⲟⲩϣⲟⲩ	m. pride 1,7
ϣⲟⲉⲓϣ	m. dust 8,18; Sa¹ 13,28
ϣϥϥⲉ	f. seventy Sa¹ 14,25
ϣⲁϫⲉ	speak, say 13,8; 16,16; Ach 41,3; 42,15; m. word 1,1
ϣⲱϫⲡ	be over, remain; m. remnant 11,23
ϥⲓ	seize, take 8,2; 10,1; 11,4; 17,11; 19,20; ϥⲓⲧ⸗ 19,9
ϥⲧⲟⲟⲩ	m. four 7,6; 11,2; 12,8(ϥⲧⲟ) ; 16,6; 19,3
ϥⲱϭⲉ	deprive 3,6
ϥⲟϭⲟⲩ	jump 9,4
ϩⲁ	prep. 8,7; 11,22*; 12,16; 17,10; 19,1*.9.11.20; ϩⲁⲣⲟ⸗ 1,10.18
ϩⲁⲉ	end 2,20; 17,17
ϩⲉ	fall 9,5; 13,3(bis); 15,16*; 19,22*.24
ϩⲉ	f. manner 4,18; 12,4.20; 20,12; ⲛⲑⲉ 1,16.17.23; 5,19; 12,12.17; 13,6; 15,17; 17,13(bis).15*.20; Sa¹ 13.28; 14,29; ⲑⲉ Ach 41,16; 42,17; 43,2
ϩⲏ	f. forepart, beginning 12,16; 13,21*; 14,2*; 19,9.11
ϩⲏ	f. stomach, body; ϩⲏⲧ⸗ 3,2; ⲛϩⲏⲧ⸗ 3,18; 4,12; 11,7; ⲛϩⲏⲧ⸗ Ach 42,9; 43,3.15
ϩⲓ	prep. 3,19; 5,13; 7,3.4(bis); 8,19; 13,21*; 14,2; 16,1.4; 17,18.22*; Sa¹ 14,13; ϩⲓⲱⲱ⸗ 4,15
ϩⲟ	f. face 7,5
ϩⲱⲱ⸗	self, also 4,18; 12,21*; 20,23

₂ⲱⲃ	m. thing; pl. ₂ⲃⲏⲩⲉ 13,14
₂ⲏⲃⲉ	f. mourning 9,20
₂ⲃⲟⲥ	m. clothing 14,12
₂ⲃⲥⲱ	f. garment 19,14
₂ⲱⲱⲕ	gird; ₂ⲟⲕ⸗ 18,5
₂ⲱⲕ	m. armour 4,15; 18,5
₂ⲕⲟ	be hungry 2,8; 19,16*
₂ⲏⲕⲉ	poor 8,12
₂ⲁⲗ	subst. with ⲉⲓⲣⲉ ; deceive 3,14
₂ⲱⲗ	fly Sa^1 14,12
₂ⲗⲗⲟ	m. old man 14,4
₂ⲁⲗⲏⲧ	m. bird; pl. ₂ⲁⲗⲉⲧⲉ 19,24*
₂ⲙⲟⲟⲥ	sit 10,3(₂ⲙⲙⲟⲟⲥ); 17,22*
₂ⲙⲟⲧ	m. grace, gift Ach 41,16
₂ⲙ₂ⲙ	roar 5,19
₂ⲙⲝ	m. vinegar 17,8
₂ⲛ	prep. *passim*; ⲉⲃⲟⲗ ₂ⲛ 1,11.20(ⲉⲃⲉⲗ); 2,1; 7,7; 9,14; 13,4; 15,16; 19,2.13
₂ⲉⲛ	indef. art. pl. *passim*
₂ⲟⲩⲛ	m. inward part; ⲉ₂ⲟⲩⲛ adv. 4,3.19; 19,12
₂ⲓⲛⲏⲃ	sleep 17,13*
₂ⲁⲡ	m. judgement Sa^1 14,30
₂ⲣⲁⲓ	m. upper part; ₂ⲣⲁⲓ ₂ⲛ 7,8; 9,9; 12,7; ⲉ₂ⲣⲁⲓ 12,6; 16,14; Sa^1 13,34(ⲁ₂₂ⲣⲁⲓ); 14,24; Ach 43,16; ⲉ₂ⲣⲁⲓ ⲉ- 7,9; 10,2.11; 11,11; 14,13; 17,1.8; 18,6.14; ⲉ₂ⲣⲁⲓ ⲉⲭⲛ- (ⲉⲭⲱ⸗) 1,14; 5,12.18; 8,12; 9,5; 14,21*; 16,13*; Sa^1 14,3; ⲉ₂ⲣⲁⲓ ₂ⲓⲭⲙ- 9,8
₂ⲣⲁⲓ	m. lower part; ⲁⲉⲡⲏⲓ Ach 42,10.11; 43.17
₂ⲣⲓⲧ	? 11,1
₂ⲣⲟⲟⲩ	m. voice 2,5; 8,16; 19,4; Sa^1 14,33
₂ⲓⲥⲉ	m. suffering 16,10
₂ⲏⲧ	m. mind, heart 4,5.19.20; 5,2; 18,15; ϣⲛ₂ⲧⲏϥ pity 1,10.18; 18,22*
₂ⲟⲉⲓⲧⲉ	f. garment 8,9; 10,15
₂ⲟⲧⲉ	f. fear 5,8
₂ⲱⲧⲃ	kill 4,16; 5,20; 7,12; 11,14.16; 16,3.15; 18,18; Sa^1 13,33; Ach 42,14 (₂ⲱⲧⲃⲉ)
₂ⲓⲧⲛ-	See ⲧⲱⲣⲉ
₂ⲱⲧⲡ	m. setting (of sun) 12,19*; 14,19*

Ⲍ ⲓⲧⲟⲟⲧ⸗	See ⲧⲱⲣ ⲉ
Ⲍⲧⲟⲟⲩⲉ	f. dawn, morning 15,17
Ⲍⲟⲟⲩ	m. day 4,4; 5,16; 6,1; 7,10.13; 8,8.10.11.15; 9,9 (bis); 10,8.18.20; 11,7.8.10; 16,2.4.6.16; 17,1*.17; 18,4.15.21; 19,18; 20,22*; Sa¹ 13,27; 14,19.31.33; Ach 41,4.9.17; 42,2.16; 43,8
Ⲍⲓⲟⲩⲉ	strike; Ⲍⲓ ⲧⲟⲟⲧ⸗ begin 6,4; 12,21(Ⲍⲟⲩ)
ⲌⲁⲌ	many Ach 42,1
Ⲍⲁⲭⲛ−, Ⲍⲓⲭⲛ−	See ⲭⲱ⸗
Ⲍⲱⲭⲡ	shut Ach 43,7(Ⲍⲱⲭⲉ?)
ⲭⲁⲉⲓⲉ	m. desert 12,1
ⲭⲉ	conj. *passim;* ⲉⲃⲟⲗ ⲭⲉ 2,16; 18,10
ⲭⲓ	take, receive 2,5; 4,13; 5,21; 6,10.12; 7,5; 8,18; 11,15; 17,18; 18,2; Sa¹ 14,11; Ach 42,13; ⲭⲓⲧ⸗ 6,15; 10,11; 19,12; ⲭⲓ ⲟⲣ to ferry 17,12; m. ferry boat 17,11
ⲭⲱ	say 1,2; 3,2; 6,16; 7,17; 9,5; 10,2.5; 12,9; 14,14; 15,3.11; 16,7.13; 17,12; 18,7.17; 20,3*.4*.22*; Sa¹ 13,23; 14,7; ⲭⲟⲟ⸗ 1,2; 6,4; 7,1; 11,20*.23; 13,2.5.19; Ach 43,4; ⲁⲭⲓⲥ imper. 1,2*
ⲭⲱ⸗	m. head 14,1*; ⲉⲭⲛ−prep. 1,4.14; 2,7; 5,12.18; 9,3; 15,1*.7; 16,14; 19,6.9.24*; Sa¹ 14,3.5; ⲉⲭⲱ⸗ 7,11; 8,12; 9,5; Ⲍⲁⲭⲱ⸗ 12,5; Ⲍⲓⲭⲛ− 6,15; 7,15; 8,6; 9,8; 10,7; 12,15; 13,5; 15,14; 17,11; 19,7.20; 20,3; Sa¹ 14,25; Ach 42,6; Ⲍⲓⲭⲱ⸗ 9,4; Ach 43,12.13
ⲭⲉⲕⲁⲁⲥ	conj. 1,11; 3,14
ⲭⲓⲛ	prep. 3,11; 9,18(ⲭⲛ) ; 19,7
ⲭⲓⲛ6ⲟⲛⲥ	m. violence 8,11
ⲭⲡⲟ	bear; ⲭⲡⲉ 10,3
ⲭⲣⲟ	be strong 17,23*
ⲭⲟⲉⲓⲥ	m. lord 2,15; ⲡⲭⲟⲉⲓⲥ 1,1.5.10; 2,6; 3,10.17; 4,1.5; 5,2.7; 11,23*; 15,5; 16,11.17; 17,14.21*; Sa¹ 14,20; Ach 42,3(ⲭⲁⲉⲓⲥ)
ⲭⲓⲥⲉ	raise up, exalt 6,6
ⲭⲟⲟⲩ	send 7,1; 13,19
ⲭⲟⲩⲱⲧ	twenty; ⲱⲙⲧⲭⲟⲩⲱⲧ sixty 18,3
ⲭⲁⲭⲉ	m. enemy 14,16; 15,13.14*; 16,18; Sa¹ 14,8
6ⲉ	then, therefore 2,1.18; 3,9; 5,1; 8,16.19*; 20.12.15; Sa¹ 13,29.31; Ach 42,10; 43,5.9
6ⲱ	remain 12,6
6ⲁⲗⲉ	lame, crippled person; pl. 6ⲁⲗⲉⲩ6ⲩ 13,7

Ϭⲱⲱⲗⲉ   swathe, clothe; Ϭⲟⲗⸯ 14,12

Ϭⲁⲗⲟⲩⲃⲓⳅ   bald-headed person 14,1

Ϭⲟⲙ   f. power, strength 13,17; 15,4; 16,16; 18,7.10; 20,6; Sa[1] 14,9(bis); ⲱ- 4,18; 17,3; 18,9; Ϭⲙ- 2,10; 5,6; 16,13; 19,17*

Ϭⲓⲛⲉ   find; Ϭⲙ- 2,10(Ϭⲛ-) ; 5,6; 6,13; 7,13; 18,9; 19,17*; 20,18.19*(Ϭⲛ-) ; Ϭⲛⲧⸯ 4,16

Ϭⲟⲛⲥ   might, violence; m. ⲭⲓⲛϬⲟⲛⲥ 8,11

Ϭⲱⲛⲧ   become angry 14,17; 15,21*; 16,20*; 17,4; 18,12 (Ϭⲟⲛⲧ) ; m. 1,5; 4,1; 19,9; Sa[1] 14,22

Ϭⲱⲡⲉ   seize, take 6,13; 7,15; 9,11.17; Ϭⲉⲡ- Sa[1] 13,32

Ϭⲣⲟⲟⲙⲡⲉ   dove 12,13.14

Ϭⲱⲣϭ   inhabit 10,12

Ϭⲟⲥ   m. half 16,4

Ϭⲓⳉ   f. hand 2,8; 4,6; 14,3; 19,7

INDEX OF PROPER NOUNS

ⲀⲤⲤⲨⲢⲒⲞⲤ	5,4.11; 11,1.14
ⲄⲀⲂⲢⲒⲎⲖ	19,10
ⲈⲚⲰⲬ	15,8; Ach 42,11
ⲒⲈⲢⲞⲨⲤⲀⲖⲎⲘ	10,11.14; 14,14; 18,6
ⲒⲞⲨⲀⲀⲒⲞⲤ	10,10
ⲒⲞⲨⲀⲀⲒⲀ	14,13
ⲔⲎⲘⲈ	5,12.21; 6,2.9; 8,10.14.18; 9,1; 10,11; 11,6.7.8
ⲔⲰⲤ	11,5
ⲘⲚϤⲈ	7,9.10; 11,5.12.13
ⲠⲈⲢⲤⲎⲤ	10,20*; 11,13.14(ⲠⲈⲢⲤⲞⲤ).21*
ⲠⲈⲢⲤⲒⲤ	10,9
ⲠⲈⲬⲢⲒⲤⲦⲞⲤ, ⲠⲈⲬⲤ	12,10.12.20*; 13,14; 17,19*; 18,18*.18.22; 19,6; 20,5.9; Ach 43,9; 44,2
ⲦⲀⲂⲒⲐⲀ	14,10
ⲞⲨⲢⲒⲎⲖ	19,10
ⳍⲎⲖⲒⲀⲤ	15,8; Ach 42,11; 44,4

Ingram Content Group UK Ltd.
Milton Keynes UK
UKHW040608280323
419285UK00001B/104